I0447240

CHINA'S POLICIES TOWARD SPIRITUAL MOVEMENTS

ROUNDTABLE

BEFORE THE

CONGRESSIONAL-EXECUTIVE COMMISSION ON CHINA

ONE HUNDRED ELEVENTH CONGRESS

SECOND SESSION

JUNE 18, 2010

Printed for the use of the Congressional-Executive Commission on China

Available via the World Wide Web: http://www.cecc.gov

U.S. GOVERNMENT PRINTING OFFICE

57–902 PDF   WASHINGTON : 2010

For sale by the Superintendent of Documents, U.S. Government Printing Office
Internet: bookstore.gpo.gov   Phone: toll free (866) 512–1800; DC area (202) 512–1800
Fax: (202) 512–2104   Mail: Stop IDCC, Washington, DC 20402–0001

CONTENTS

CHINA'S POLICIES TOWARD SPIRITUAL MOVEMENTS

FRIDAY, JUNE 18, 2010

CONGRESSIONAL-EXECUTIVE
COMMISSION ON CHINA,
Washington, DC.

The roundtable was convened, pursuant to notice, at 2:03 p.m., in room 628, Dirksen Senate Office Building, Douglas Grob (Cochairman's Senior Staff Member), presiding.

OPENING STATEMENT OF DOUGLAS GROB, COCHAIRMAN'S SENIOR STAFF MEMBER, CONGRESSIONAL-EXECUTIVE COMMISSION ON CHINA

Mr. GROB. Good afternoon, ladies and gentlemen, and thank you very much for joining us here today. On behalf of Senator Byron Dorgan, Chairman, and Representative Sander Levin, Cochairman, and Charlotte Oldham-Moore, Staff Director of the Congressional-Executive Commission on China [CECC], I would like to welcome you to this, the 14th Congressional-Executive Commission on China roundtable held during the 111th Congress.

My name is Douglas Grob and I am Cochairman Levin's Senior Staff Member.

We have asked our distinguished panelists here today to examine the Chinese Government's policies toward spiritual movements and the factors that drive Chinese Government officials' treatment of members of spiritual groups. The Chinese Government has allowed space for some spiritual movements to operate in China, but the Communist Party has banned other groups, such as the popular spiritual movement, Falun Gong. Authorities have subjected members of Falun Gong and other banned groups to strict surveillance and, in some cases, imprisonment, detention outside the legal system, and other abuses. Why does the Chinese Government consider some spiritual movements a threat, and what challenges and prospects do Falun Gong practitioners face in China that adherents of other groups may not? And what does the Chinese Government's treatment of spiritual movements mean for religious freedom in China?

We still do not have a clear understanding of all the factors that prompt Chinese authorities to criminalize some spiritual movements as "cult" organizations.

We will hear today of individuals subjected to abuse, in some cases including detention and imprisonment. These cases include those of Wang Chunyan, Qiu Shaojie, Cao Junping, Tian Zhongxia, Zhu Lijin, Li Yaohua, Chen Zhenping, Qiao Yongfang, and Yan

Dongfei. Other cases, some less well known, include the cases of Xu Na, Wang Zhiwen, Yang Xiyao, Zhang Binglan, Duan Youru, Li Zongbo, and others. These are Falun Gong practitioners, but there are cases of members of other spiritual movements labeled as cults in China as well, including Shi Hua, Gong Shengliang, Tong Houyong, Shu Wenxiang, Xie Zhenqi, and others.

Another case that we will hear about today is that of Gao Zhisheng, a prominent Chinese human rights attorney who, in late March 2010, resurfaced after having disappeared for more than a year and who has now again disappeared. Gao's case has attracted international attention due in part to his legal advocacy on behalf of religious minorities, including Falun Gong practitioners, Christians, and ethnic minorities, rural farmers, and human rights advocates. A self-taught lawyer, Gao Zhisheng repeatedly has angered Chinese authorities by taking on case that authorities deem to be "sensitive," and by exposing human rights abuses.

It is worth noting what both international human rights standards and provisions in Chinese law say about the rights of members of spiritual movements.

The Universal Declaration of Human Rights, Article 18, says,

Everyone has the right to freedom of thought, conscience, and religion. This right includes freedom to change his religion or belief and freedom, either alone or in community with others, and in public or private, to manifest his religion or belief in teaching, practice, worship, and observance.

Article 19 says,

Everyone has the right to freedom of opinion and expression, and this right includes freedom to hold opinions without interference and to seek, receive, and impart information and ideas through any media and regardless of frontiers.

Article 20 says,

Everyone has the right to freedom of peaceful assembly and association.

The International Covenant on Civil and Political Rights, Article 18, says,

Everyone shall have the right to freedom of thought, conscience, and religion. This right shall include freedom to have or to adopt a religion or belief of his choice, and freedom, either individually or in community with others, and in public or private, to manifest his religions or belief in worship, observance, practice, and teaching. No one shall be subject to coercion which would impair his freedom to have or to adopt a religion or belief of his choice. Freedom to manifest one's religion or beliefs may be subject only to such limitations as are prescribed by law and are necessary to protect public safety, order, health, or morals, or the fundamental rights and freedoms of others. The State Parties to the present Covenant undertake to have respect for the liberty of parents and, when applicable, legal guardians to ensure the religious and moral education of their children in conformity with their own convictions.

The Constitution of the People's Republic of China, Article 35, states,

Citizens of the People's Republic of China enjoy freedom of speech, of the press, of assembly, of association, of procession, and of demonstration.

Article 36 of the Constitution of the People's Republic of China states,

Citizens of the People's Republic of China enjoy freedom of religious belief. No state organ, public organization, or individual may compel citizens to believe in or not to believe in any religion, nor may they discriminate against citizens who believe in or do not believe in any religion. The state protects normal religious activities. No one may make use of religion to engage in activities that disrupt public order, impair the health of citizens, or interfere with the educational system of the state. Religious bodies and religious affairs are not subject to any foreign domination.

With that in mind, it is my great pleasure to introduce our panelists today. James Tong, professor, UCLA Department of Political Science, and chief editor of the Journal of Chinese Law and Government. Professor Tong previously served as the vice chairman of UCLA's Department of Political Science and director of UCLA's Center for East Asian Studies. His publications include "Revenge of the Forbidden City: The Suppression of the Falun Gong in China, 1999–2000," and a number of articles and edited volumes on central and provincial religious policy documents in China, ethnic conflict, and the 1989 democracy movement in Beijing. He has served as a World Bank consultant, briefed the U.S. Commission on International Religious Freedom, and has participated in a previous CECC roundtable on religious regulations, and we're very pleased to have you back here today.

Ethan Gutmann, to my left, is Adjunct Fellow at the Foundation for Defense of Democracies. He is currently completing a comprehensive history of the clash between Falun Gong and the Chinese State, and in addition has begun preliminary research into, quote, "the Chinese Uyghur conflict and the underlying ambiguity of the Chinese Communist Party's stance toward the Islamist global challenge." He is the author of, "Losing the New China: A Story of American Commerce, Desire, and Betrayal." He is formerly a senior counselor at APCO China and a visiting fellow at the Project for the New American Century. He has written widely on Chinese military development, human rights, the U.S. business scene in Beijing, and on recent hacking for the Wall Street Journal, Investor's Business Daily, The Weekly Standard, and a number of other prominent publications. We are very delighted to have you here today.

To my right is Mark Shan, of the Program in Philosophy, Theology and Ethics at Boston University. Mr. Shan has written about the house church movement in China, focusing on Christian theology and social ethics. He has published two books, "The Future Direction of Churches in China," and "The History of Christianity in Xinjiang." He also serves as consultant on religious and political issues in China for organizations in the United States, and he is the primary founder of a newly established Chinese Christian Theology Association based in Boston. Originally from Xinjiang, China,

Mr. Shan now resides in Boston where he is pursuing his Christian theological studies at Boston University, and we are delighted to have you with us today.

Also to my right is Sarah Cook, Asia Research Analyst at Freedom House, and assistant editor for the "Freedom on the Net" index on Internet and digital media freedom. She has served as East Asia Analyst for Freedom House's "Freedom of the Press" and "Freedom in the World" reports. Her research has covered human rights and media developments in East Asia, Indochina, and the Middle East, including fact-finding trips to Hong Kong and Taiwan. Her comments and writings have appeared on CNN, the International Herald Tribune, and the Far Eastern Economic Review. Before joining Freedom House, she co-edited the English translation of "A China More Just," a memoir by human rights attorney Gao Zhisheng. She was twice a delegate to the United Nations Human Rights Commission meeting in Geneva, working on religious freedom in China, and she is currently completing an article on the Chinese Communist Party's creation and use of the 6–10 Office to suppress Falun Gong and other banned spiritual groups.

All of our panelists' statements are on the table outside and will be available online. I would also like to take this opportunity to call your attention to an additional statement, also available on the table outside, by Ms. Caylan Ford, who is here with us today, a volunteer with the Falun Dafa Information Center. This statement has been submitted for the record and will be available to the public with the other statements from this roundtable.

With that, I would like to turn the floor over to Professor Tong. Thank you.

Professor Tong?

[The prepared statement of Ms. Ford appears in the appendix.]

STATEMENT OF JAMES TONG, PROFESSOR, DEPARTMENT OF POLITICAL SCIENCE, UNIVERSITY OF CALIFORNIA–LOS ANGELES

Mr. TONG. My talk today will be on how the Chinese regime views the threat posed by the Falun Gong in recent years, and also how it differentiates different types of Falun Gong members and offenses that they impose legal and also political sanctions, and also a few remarks on the implications on the larger issues on religious freedom in China.

On July 22, 1999, when China announced a ban on Falun Gong, there were between 2.3 million to about 80 million Falun Gong practitioners in China. This wide range results from the fact that there is no clear and formal definition of a Falun Gong practitioner because, unlike Christians, the Falun Gong has no rite of formal induction into the religious community. Different levels of Falun Gong organizations also do not maintain a membership roster, so there is no accurate count on the number of Falun Gong practitioners in China before the ban of July 22, 1999.

These Falun Gong practitioners were organized into about 28,000 practice sites throughout China and they were further grouped into about 1,900 guidance stations, and further grouped into about 39 main stations. Every morning, they would gather together in the city parks and other public places for breathing exercises.

Since July 22, 1999, these breathing exercises and daily assemblies have virtually disappeared. Also disappeared were the special convocations. These were larger congregations that the Falun Gong practitioners gathered together on special congregational anniversaries, and also training seminars lasting three to four days, where they learned special breathing exercises, meditation techniques, and also Falun Gong doctrine.

These three public forums of organized activities of the Falun Gong movement in China have been successfully and effectively suppressed in China, and so have been their publications. On July 22, 1999, there were at least 11 million copies of Falun Gong publications. They belonged to about 11 Falun Gong titles. These were confiscated.

On the seventh day of the ban, on July 29, they were collected together and set ablaze or turned into paper pulp in 17 major cities in China. In sum, the Chinese regime has been effective in suppressing the public forms of organized activities of the Falun Gong movement in China.

There still have been periodic reports of overt defiance by Falun Gong practitioners in China. These include the staging of protest rallies in the national and provincial capitals, displaying the banner of the Falun Gong in public, and also engaging in sabotage of media organizations in China, but these have been rare in China in at least the past seven or eight years.

There are three related developments that demonstrate that fact. The first is the annual report of the chief procurator in China. This is the equivalent to the Attorney General of the United States. Every year, the annual procurator report would list what are the major law enforcement problems in China in that year. In the first five years of the ban on Falun Gong, from 1999 to 2003, the Falun Gong was listed as one of the major law enforcement problems in China, but it has no longer made that list since 2004.

Below the national level, each of the provincial procurators would also make an annual report that mirrors largely the national trend. So in 1999, the procurator of 29 of the 31 provinces mentioned that the Falun Gong was a major law enforcement problem in that province in that year; in 2000, 28 provinces; 2001, 21 provinces; and since then, there has been a precipitous decline. In 2004, there were only seven provinces, and in 2008 there were only two provinces where the provincial procurator list the Falun Gong as a serious, major law enforcement issue in that province.

The second related development is the end to the followup and mopping-up operations conducted by the regime. Since the initial blitz in July 1999, there was a second followup campaign in the summer of 2001 where, for four months, the public security agents would fan out and try to ferret out fugitive Falun Gong leaders. They would try to locate where the hideouts were. They would also try to search and confiscate Falun Gong publications.

In addition, some provinces conducted single-day operations on Falun Gong special days. And in some strong Falun Gong hold-outs there were 100-day campaigns where public security agents would systematically go through all Internet cafes, printing presses, photocopying vendors, and rental properties to try to locate Falun

Gong practitioners and inventories of Falun Gong publications. None of these followup campaigns have been reported since 2003.

Then the third development is the reorganization of the special agency dealing with the Falun Gong. Forty days before the official ban on July 22, the June 10 office was established at different levels of government, both at the national and at local levels. Their business was exclusively to deal with the Falun Gong.

In April 2002, these offices' mission was broadened to include not only other spiritual movements and cults, but also collective protests and rallies organized by non-religious groups, including, workers who are on strike, and demonstrating peasants who were evicted from their farmland.

In other words, all three developments combined suggest that by 2003 or 2004, the Chinese regime did not see the Falun Gong as a major law enforcement problem and a security threat posed to the regime.

My second set of remarks are focused on what type of Falun Gong practitioners and what type of offenses the regime deemed unacceptable, that it levied the legal and political sanctions.

Let me begin with a reiteration of the basic fact that there were at least 2.3 million Falun Gong practitioners in China in July 1999. That is four times the total population of Washington, DC. If we take the largest estimate, 80 million Falun Gong practitioners, that is about a quarter of the total population of the United States. There is no way that the Chinese regime had the judicial capacity to process all these cases.

In 1998, the year just before the ban, the entire judicial system in China handled only 400,000 criminal cases that involved 600,000 individuals. If we look at only the three major offenses that the Chinese State charged Falun Gong practitioners with, these include offenses that endanger the state security, endangering the social order, and obstructing social order. In 1998, the judicial system in China only processed 74,000 of these cases. At this rate, it would have taken them 31 years just to clear 2.3 million cases. So they have to differentiate on what types of Falun Gong members they will levy legal sanctions.

On the same day that they announced the ban, they differentiated them into four different categories. The first type are the rank and file Falun Gong practitioners who have only participated in breathing exercises. For these, no legal sanction was levied.

The other three types were core members who have committed illegal activities. If they would renounce the Falun Gong, write a written statement stating their official withdrawal from the Falun Gong, and also render an account of their activities, there was also no legal and political sanction. For political sanction, if they are a government official, or work in a government enterprise, they would not be dismissed, they would not be demoted, their year-end bonus would not be cut, their benefits would not be affected. If they are a member of the Chinese Communist Party, they will not be expelled from the Party. As for legal sanction, if they have broken a law, but would renounce the Falun Gong, and withdraw from the Falun Gong, they would not be prosecuted, according to that formal announcement.

The next category are core leaders who have committed serious errors, that is, they have facilitated the organizing of the protests or they have distributed, or even printed, illegal Falun Gong publications. If they renounce the Falun Gong and withdraw from Falun Gong, if they would also make a conscientious confession, and accrue merit, that is, if they would persuade other Falun Gong members to withdraw from Falun Gong, if they would point out who are the Falun Gong leaders, if they would incriminate these leaders, if they would tell the authorities where the publications are hidden, then they would also receive no sanction.

The last type were what the Chinese regime considered to be unrepentant core leaders who have committed serious mistakes. These are the ones who would receive political and legal sanctions. If they have violated what the Chinese State considered to be laws, then they would be prosecuted, they would be incarcerated or sent to labor reform.

My last remarks are on the implications for religious freedom in China. Religion in China is still a managed religion. The Chinese State claims the authority to define what is religion and what is not religion, what is a religious organization, and what is a cult. It also claims the authority to define what is normal religious activity from what is considered to be illegal religious activity. At every level of government there is a religious affairs bureau that manages the religious affairs within its jurisdiction.

But this capacity to manage religion has been eroded by market reforms. On the supply side, market reform has created political space where spiritual movements can survive outside the control of the Party state. In the Maoist era, virtually the entire working population worked for government-owned enterprises. They lived in government-owned housing. They relied on government-issued food and clothing coupons. But that is no longer the case under market reforms. These spiritual movements can now find alternative means of employment in the non-state sector. There is a housing market. The ration coupons have also ended.

On the demand side, market reforms have also created social conflict that the Chinese Government needs to attend to. It is not only the rising crime wave that the procurator at both the national and provincial levels stress. These are organized crime, robberies, bank heists, and drug trafficking. There is also the rising wave of collective protests.

In 1994, there were 10,000 of these collective protests. These are unemployed workers, workers who do not receive pensions, People's Liberation Army [PLA] soldiers that have been discharged with minimum severance pay. These groups have staged collective protests. In 1994, there were 10,000, about 30 incidents per year. But 10 years later in 2004, there were 74,000 of these collective protests. In one month alone, in May 2004, there were 2,180 of these collective protests, and each one had participants of 500 or more.

So when compared to these collective protests and the crime wave with people demonstrating in the streets or outside the government offices, both the Falun Gong as well as other spiritual movements would be viewed as rather tame in the eyes of the Chinese regime.

Finally, market reform has also made religious policy a collateral beneficiary. In the Maoist era, there was a convergence of religious policy with overall political, economic, and social policies. But 30 years into the market reform, there is a divergence between religious policy on the one hand and the political, economic, and social policy on the other.

China today is no longer a Communist State. The major Communist anniversaries are no longer celebrated. The 150th anniversary of the publication of the Communist Manifesto has no People's Daily editorial. The 90th anniversary of the Bolshevik Revolution is not celebrated.

China is not a Leninist economy where there is no private ownership of production and where there are no labor and capitalists markets. Today there are 150 million account holders in the Shanghai and Shenzhen Stock Exchanges. When we compare 150 million account holders with 72 million Chinese Communist Party members, we can say that there are at least twice as many capitalists as Communist members in China.

In other words, there is divergence between the religious policy and overall political, economic, and social policy in China today. The Chinese regime has to bridge this divergence. It has to adjust its clock in religious policy so that it will be run on the same time zone as the political, economic, and social policy.

So on this note, I will conclude my set of remarks. Thank you.

[The prepared statement of Mr. Tong appears in the appendix.]

Mr. GROB. Thank you very much, Professor Tong. Thank you so much.

I would now like to turn the floor over to Ethan Gutmann.

STATEMENT OF ETHAN GUTMANN, ADJUNCT FELLOW, FOUNDATION FOR DEFENSE OF DEMOCRACIES

Mr. GUTMANN. Thanks. I want to thank the CECC, but my remarks need to go beyond the pro forma on this point. The Chinese Communist Party portrays Falun Gong as an evil cult and as a terrorist entity. The Chinese State's diplomatic arm has made it clear that the Falun Gong issue is non-negotiable. It is relevant that this appears to be the first U.S. Government hearing or roundtable directly focusing on Falun Gong in a decade.

As a former Beijing business consultant, I do not rely on Chinese official statistics. For example, if you attempt to generate a population figure for the *laogai* system—labor camps, prisons, black jails, detention centers, and psychiatric hospitals—you get a figure well below a million. Yet if one counts every detention node and makes common-sense estimates, as Laogai Foundation researchers do every year, you get a more credible figure of 3 to 5 million.

According to the U.N. Rapporteur on Torture, Falun Gong comprises half of those prisoners, but this figure might be high. Much of my research is based on interviews with refugees and defectors. I do not ask them for estimates of the *laogai* system, but no matter how traumatized they are, I do expect them to remember how many Falun Gong were in their cell block.

After interviewing over 120 individuals, including defectors from inside Chinese security and well over 50 *laogai* refugees, I estimate that Falun Gong comprises between 15 to 20 percent of the *laogai* system. That is about half a million to a million Falun Gong in detention on average, representing the largest Chinese security action since the Maoist period.

Now we often perceive China's human rights problems as an entrenched structure, something similar to how Solzhenitsyn describes the Soviet gulag as a large plumbing system. But the Party's campaign against Falun Gong more closely resembles a blitzkrieg in an increasingly global war, marked by physical assaults in the United States—and I'm happy to talk about this—Chinese operatives posing as refugees, and coordinated hacking of Chinese dissident networks and U.S. Government entities.

We should understand how that war began, we should understand the casualty rates, and we should understand the stakes of our neutrality. So I thank the CECC again, and especially Toy Reid, for making this roundtable a reality.

I was in Beijing on July 20—really, July 22, I think, as Professor Tong points out—1999 when the official crackdown began and sound trucks flooded the streets. Western reporters were flooding the zone, but they had little cooperation from either the Party or Falun Gong at the time, so journalists had trouble simply penciling in the first question of any news report: What is Falun Gong?

Falun Gong, simply put, is a Buddhist revival movement. It has moral passion, it has occasional talk of miracles, it has "Are you running with Me, Master Li?" individualism, and it has a reflexive mistrust of establishments and outsider agendas.

This Buddhist aspect may be unfamiliar and exotic in the West, but as Arthur Waldron puts it: "Anyone who knows Asian religion will instantly see that Falun Gong fits into a tradition that extends back before the beginning of recorded history." What made Falun Gong stand out from other Qi Gong exercises and meditation practices was a moral system—compassion, truthfulness, and forbearance—unmistakably Buddhist in origin.

The revivalist aspect helps explain why Falun Gong insists on being called practitioners rather than followers. Actually, they don't follow well. If you ask 10 Falun Gong practitioners for a definition of Falun Gong, you will get 10 different answers and probably 10 days of heated discussions. Yet it was that same do-it-yourself mentality that allowed Falun Gong to attract 70 million practitioners—according to the 6–10 Office—and skip over the barriers of Chinese society: class, education, rural/urban, civilian/military, and Party membership.

Go back to 1995 and follow a diminutive old woman around Yuan Ming Park in West Beijing. Ding Jing was a Falun Gong coordinator, meaning she taught the exercises, and she kept practice sites clean. Among the sites were three locations. One catered to employees from China Central Television; two, the Xinhua News Agency; and three—very well attended—attracted Party officials, their wives, and employees of the Public Security Bureau.

From a Marxist perspective, which venerates the seizure of power using this exact template, Ding's tidy practice sites represented something terrifying. In 1996, "Zhuan Falun," in essence the Falun Gong bible, was taken out of print.

Given the amorphous, floating world in which practitioners traveled—largely perceived as amorphous and floating anyway—a world without membership lists, central authority, or any real hierarchy other than on paper, practitioners did not panic. But Luo Gan, the head of the Public Security Bureau, began to use Falun Gong's perceived infiltration of his own department to gather, to report, and to study. Where no hierarchy existed, the Party, seizing on small clues such as Ding's phone calls, would map one. Where no political objectives existed, the Party would create them.

Until 1997, the Chinese media stayed neutral. Local Party leaders would show up at Falun Dafa rallies. Now critical language began to appear in the Party-controlled media. These were flares in the night's sky, indicating the Party was trying something out. The Falun Gong had a method to handle this: Show up en masse, stay silent, and then stand around until someone talks to you. This technique smoothly reversed the various negative reports, articles in 1997, a Beijing TV segment in 1998. In Tianjin in 1999—it failed.

Now, I do not know if the article has been handed out yet, but you can certainly find it on the Web if it has not made it here, and you may be able to pick it up on the way out: "An Occurrence on Fuyou Street." Employing interviews from both sides, my article tracks the events from Xinjiang on April 22 to Beijing on April 25, 1999. Essentially, the demonstration was a set-up. From the portable surveillance cameras on Fuyou Street to the armed military unit at the Forbidden City, it was a Party bait-and-switch to create momentum for a state-level crackdown.

A former district-level official—"Minister X," that's what I call him—recalls the Party's decision to eliminate Falun Gong was circulated internally long before any public ban, and he was told to stop granting business licenses to Falun Gong practitioners. A Falun Gong source saw a similar communiqué at Tsinghua University in 1998. A former official of the 6–10 Office—the secret agency created to eliminate Falun Gong—noting the level of detail in practitioner files, believes that operations must have begun by at least 1998.

Without understanding the initial integration of Falun Gong into the Party and the Party's initiative in starting the war—essentially creating the dilemma that threatens the Party today—one cannot understand the ineffectiveness of the Falun Gong response. Practitioners wanted to believe that it was a misunderstanding. So practitioner appearances at the petition office and signed letters were followed by mass detentions and the first deaths in custody.

Beginning in 2000, based on the safe house occupancy in Beijing, I estimate that well over 150,000 practitioners made their way into Tiananmen Square to protest over a year's time. Collectively, that is a remarkable number. But they trickled in at 500 to 1,000 per day, and they stood up and unfurled their banners according to the dictates of their soul rather than any sort of preconceived strategy.

Would a mass strategy even have been possible? Well, I have provided another article—"Hacker Nation"—on 6–10 surveillance:

> Before 1999, Falun Gong practitioners hadn't systematically used the Internet as an organizing tool. But now that they were isolated, fragmented, and searching for a way to organize and change government policy, they jumped online, employing code words, avoiding specifics, communicating in short bursts.

But like a cat listening to mice squeak in a pitch-black house, the "Internet Spying" section of the 6–10 Office could find their exact location, having developed the ability to search and spy as a result of . . . a joint venture between the Shandong Province public security bureau, and Cisco Systems.

That's right out of my article, and there is a lot more in there as well.

Following capture and initial interrogation under the 6–10 Office, the *laogai* system then operated to break the will and "transform" the practitioner, culminating with a public denunciation of Falun Gong. But it was within the *laogai* itself that the first effective resistance began.

Wang Yuzhi was a tough, successful Beijing businesswoman. And when the crackdown started she transformed her office into a secret Falun Gong printing press. It was broken up, her assets were seized, Wang ran, and was eventually caught.

The low-ball casualty figure of over 3,000 practitioners who have died by torture is reasonably well-documented. Some practitioners simply refused to renounce their belief, others hoped that the overcrowded prisons might contribute to the end of the persecution, and others wanted to just set an example to fellow inmates.

But Wang made it personal, so personal that some of the guards force-feeding her began wearing paper bag masks so she could not identify them. It became a chess game between the practitioner and the torturers. Both sides knew that Wang's screams of rage were becoming legendary throughout the *laogai* System, and indeed, to practitioners throughout the world. Both sides knew that checkmate, actually killing Wang, would leave a pyrrhic victory for the state.

The underlying ambiguity of the *laogai* position was expressed in the following maneuver. Rather than writing up a report of transformation failure, or the euphemism "death by suicide," many labor camps and psychiatric centers would wait until the torture reached lethal levels and then suddenly free the dying practitioner—especially after the so-called Tiananmen self-immolation and the Changchun television hijacking and I would welcome questions on those incidents.

But Wang Yuzhi lived. Considered terminal on release, she fled China and went on to purchase printing presses for The Epoch Times. Today she will smile at you with her one good eye. This is the face of insurgency, and to such a face, the Party turned toward a more permanent solution.

The final article that I have made available, "China's Gruesome Organ Harvest," documents a pattern of retail-organs-only physical examinations carried out throughout the *laogai* system. I can find no rational medical explanation for these procedures, and I conclude that the commercial harvesting of Falun Gong is real. That finding has since been confirmed by a Taiwanese surgeon who arranges transplants on the Mainland.

One addition. While the Bush Administration's consistent focus on house Christians may have had a "Schindler's List" effect, inhibiting widespread harvesting of Christians, members of at least one sect, Eastern Lightening, were examined for harvesting. According to interviews by my colleague Jaya Gibson, so were some Tibetan prisoners.

Yet harvesting of political and religious prisoners probably began in Xinjiang. A Uyghur policeman witnessed preparation for a procedure in 1994, and I recently interviewed a Uyghur surgeon who, in 1995, was ordered to take his medical team into the outskirts of Urumqi and remove a prisoner's organs while the heart was still beating.

Perhaps harvesting began as a purely black-market operation, but ultimately prisoners who would not transform—the Wang Yuzhis of this world, if you like—became too dangerous to release. But the Party had an outlet, the organ tourists of Japan, Europe, and the United States.

Now, the fact that China is the one currently pulling up the reins on Western organ tourism highlights Falun Gong's stunning lack of success in making its case in the United States. I mean, one would expect that it would be Congress who would be preventing organ tourists from going over to China, but it's not. It's the Party, and they seem to be pulling back on organ harvesting.

Let me explain what I think happened in the United States. For many in the Bush Administration at least, it took one outburst from Wang Wenyi on the White House lawn to establish that Falun Gong could never be reliable allies. For many Democrats, it took one Chinese-planted Wikipedia reference alleging Falun Gong was anti-gay to ward off sympathy. Yet Falun Gong teachings on this point are essentially indistinguishable from traditional Christianity, Judaism, Islam, and Buddhism.

Practitioners have some responsibility here, too. In the West, they simultaneously watch two screens. They watch a Western one and they watch a Chinese one. But for them, China is always the default. And fear of the Party's manipulative abilities on that screen run very deep indeed. Hence, we see the definitional problems, we see the alienating public torture displays and the rest, and we see Daoist demarcations of good and evil. Again, all of these are aimed at the Mainland.

Yet Falun Gong's tunnel vision did create one unprecedented success. Along with the construction of the greatest dissident media apparatus in modern Chinese history, a small group of Falun Gong engineers, based out of a North Carolina suburb, devised an Internet lifeline to transmit information in and out of China. Along the way, they facilitated the only unblocked Internet transmissions out of Iran during the aborted Green Revolution.

If the press is correct, the State Department is considering awarding these engineers, now known as the Global Internet Freedom Consortium, significant funding to do more. If my Falun Gong sources are correct, the Consortium is concerned about taking a sum too small to make a difference, in exchange for the inevitable Party propaganda point that they are now U.S. agents.

Yet the Party is pushing the two sides together. The State Department must end Chinese hacking, and the only way State can do it is by threatening China's Big Brother Internet. Falun Gong has perhaps a half a million to a million in captivity; as much as 1 out of 10 Falun Gong may have already been lost to the surgical knife.

So the answer to this dilemma will not be found in parsing Wikipedia. And the question is no longer—"What is Falun Gong and how do they define themselves?" But rather—"What are Falun Gong's actions? What has the Falun Gong achieved? Against what sort of odds?" And here, I believe that the evidence of a decade, from the *laogai* to the North Carolina suburbs, speaks for itself.

[The prepared statement of Mr. Gutmann appears in the appendix.]

Mr. GROB. Thank you very much.

Mr. Shan?

STATEMENT OF MARK SHAN, PROGRAM IN PHILOSOPHY, THEOLOGY AND ETHICS, BOSTON UNIVERSITY

Mr. SHAN. Good afternoon, ladies and gentlemen, CECC members, staff, and interns.

The roundtable host, the CECC, asked the question, "What factors influence the Chinese Government's policies toward spiritual movements and drive its treatment of members of spiritual groups? The Chinese Government has allowed space for some spiritual movements to operate in China, but has banned other groups such as Falun Gong. Why does the Chinese Government consider some spiritual movements a threat?"

These questions touch the root of Chinese political/religious culture. My following remarks are trying to find out a rationale behind these policies, yet have no intention to justify the policies.

For a better understanding, first I need to introduce a concept in traditional Chinese political ideology which influenced throughout the history of China, and that is "the Mandate of Heaven." The concept officially started by the Zhou Dynasty in 11th century B.C. to justify their replacement of the Shang Dynasty.

Because the concept justified all successful overthrows, just as it justified all dynasties that clung to power, the concept has lasting influence and has even survived into modern and contemporary China. For instance, in the modern period, a famous revolution was called The Kingdom of Heavenly Peace Movement, led by Hong Xiuquan in the middle of the 19th century. Again in the modern time, another man, Sun Zhongshan, famous for leading a revolution against the Qing Dynasty, also can reflect this kind of concept.

Because of the spiritual feature of this political concept, spiritual or religious movements in Chinese history make it easy to challenge the ruling of dynasties through spiritual and moral approaches. So the Chinese Governments have been sensitive throughout its history to the political/spiritual touch and are not tolerant of any spiritual movements shaking their ruling authority, before the Chinese people especially.

In addition, Chinese Governments have tended to keep state and religion separated through promoting a non-religious system, Confucianism, throughout much of their history. Indeed, this is an efficient way to keep religious or spiritual movements out of politics.

Throughout Chinese history, all the Chinese Governments set up this forbidden area: do not touch politics. Do not play around with the concept of the Mandate of Heaven. The only politics you can touch are the politics that support rulings of government. So based on the understanding of this concept, we can find out the rationale behind the political religious policy of China today, which is why the Chinese Government treats different spiritual movements differently.

For example, the Protestant Christian house churches and the Catholic underground house churches. They are persecuted, but the Protestant and the Catholic churches that are officially public through the Three-Self Patriotic System [TSPM] enjoy more freedom.

Tibetan Buddhism is under suppression because of its feature of the religion/politics combination in its doctrine and tradition. But Buddhism and Daoism in other parts of China enjoy much more freedom because they touch no politics. Islam among Uyghurs is under suppression because of the Xinjiang political situation, the problems there, but Islam among Hui people enjoys more freedom.

This is true not only inside the same spiritual traditions or religious traditions, but also if we compare government's treatments among different spiritual movements or religions in China.

Now we are going to talk about the Falun Gong movement. The Falun Gong movement was suppressed a lot, as Mr. Tong and Ethan mentioned. Actually the Falun Gong movement is only one branch of the Qi Gong, but the Falun Gong even was suppressed more than other Qi Gong branches. So, why? Because on April 25, 1999, the siege of the Chinese Communist Party headquarters in Beijing by the Falun Gong movement members, more than 20,000, really touched the nerve of politics.

We also see, after the Falun Gong movement went abroad here, there is one famous slogan from the Falun Gong movement. It says, "Heaven eliminates the Chinese Communist Party," encouraging people to withdraw from the Communist Party. This is another interpretation of the concept of the Mandate of Heaven.

So that is why a human rights Christian lawyer in China, Gao Zhisheng, has received the most serious, inhumane persecutions, even compared to other persecuted lawyers, because he is trying to defend religious freedom and the human rights of some Falun Gong practitioners.

The CECC also asked another question: "What does the Chinese Government's treatments of the spiritual movement mean for the future of religious freedom in China?"

This is another interesting question. A sociologist, Dr. Yang Fenggang, proposed a triple color model that analyzes the religious situation in contemporary China. Through this formula we can see that he divided three markets: the red market, which means official, permitted religions; a black market means officially banned religions; and a gray market, religions with ambiguous legal status. Through this formula we can pretty much answer this question from this perspective.

The red market means religious or spiritual movements which do not touch on politics, so they have the most freedom, like non-Tibetan Buddhism and Daoism. A black market religious market means the banned ones, such as the Falun Gong movement and some branches of Islam in Xinjiang—some branches—which touch on politics, challenging the Communist Party authority; so they have the most suppression.

The gray market, which is ambiguous in their political interest, are things such as non-institutionalized Protestant house church entities. The Catholic underground church is a little bit different because they are closer to the black market because of the political feature extending from the Vatican court.

The gray market of the non-institutional house church movement has grown large and will grow larger, when others are encouraged or suppressed. Of course, there is a dilemma. If this house church movement, the gray market, grows really large, then it becomes more political.

In China, also, this kind of house church movement, the people, they are trying to deal with the policies in a unique way. So in church settings in China, they focus on teachings, like Biblical teachings, such as "Blessed are those who are persecuted," "Love your enemy and even love the persecutors." Also, they emphasize in their teachings that they do not touch politics. They do not touch politics. The president of ChinaAid, Bob Fu, was arrested in Beijing and was trying to argue, we do not touch politics; we support church/state separation; something like that.

But of course, China is trying to suppress the house church movements and its Christians too, because they learn lessons from Eastern Europe. When those Communist countries collapsed, Christianity played an indirect role.

So together, I think in China, Christianity, in the gray market and also even in the red market, TSPM churches, they are going to transform the condition of religious freedom in China significantly in the future, especially through something we call the new non-institutionalized religious citizen community, established in the whole nation, but it is not kind of an hierarchical, administrative, visible system.

Those are my remarks.

[The prepared statement of Mr. Shan appears in the appendix.]

Mr. GROB. Thank you very much, Mr. Shan.

And now, finally, we'd like to hear from Sarah Cook. Thank you.

STATEMENT OF SARAH COOK, ASIA RESEARCH ANALYST, FREEDOM HOUSE

Ms. COOK. Good afternoon, everyone. One of the topics I was asked to speak about is the story of Gao Zhisheng, who you can see here [holds up copy of "A China More Just"]. As Doug had mentioned, he's a leading Chinese human rights lawyer and has been a vocal advocate for religious freedom in China, particularly of Falun Gong practitioners.

Several years ago, I had the real honor of co-editing this English edition of his memoir, and so as I was thinking about how I would begin today, I tried to think about what Gao would say if he were here himself. He has disappeared, as Doug had mentioned, so that is why he can't be here today. I think the first thing he would say is a real heart-felt thank you.

First, thank you to the Commission for organizing this panel, thank you to the U.S. Government for taking an active interest in the human rights abuses happening to Chinese people, and thank you to all of you in the audience who are here to listen to what the four of us have to say.

Second, I think he would likely try to convey the real urgency of the current situation and the ongoing brutality of the treatment suffered by large numbers of Chinese people generally, but of Falun Gong practitioners in particular. One of the things that is very clear from his writings is that account after account after account of torture that he heard while interviewing Falun Gong practitioners left a very profound impression on him and really served as a catalyst for his taking the risks that he has taken in order to defend them.

So I am just going to briefly read a short portion from one of the things he had written:

> With a trembling heart and a trembling pen, I record the tragic experiences of those who have been persecuted in the last six years. Of all the true accounts of incredible violence that I have heard, of all the records of the government's inhuman torture of its own people, what has shaken me most is the routine practice of police assaulting women's genitals. Almost all those who have been persecuted, be they male or female, were stripped naked before being tortured. No words can describe our government's vulgarity and immorality.

Now, while not spoken in quite such detailed and colorful language, Freedom House's findings generally correlate to what Gao had found. But before I move on to some of the specific details that have arisen from our reports over the last 10 years, I did want to take a step back to address a slightly different angle about why this kind of suppression might take place. It doesn't, indeed, happen in a vacuum.

Rather, what has been happening to Falun Gong and spiritual movements who are banned in China is really part of a much broader, elaborate machinery of repression that systematically tries to control and deny independent thought and expression in a range of areas throughout Chinese society. In many ways, Freedom House's reports in recent years have found that this repression has been getting worse in certain areas.

As Professor Tong had mentioned, the dynamic in China right now is very different from what it was like during the Cultural Revolution. But some of the underlying principles and institutional dynamics remain the same in the sense that the decision of what is approved or forbidden can be made arbitrarily by Party leaders based on their own perceptions of the threats to their monopoly on power or legitimacy, whether these threats are real or imagined.

As someone who follows Chinese media very closely, I see this dynamic played out on a day-to-day basis with the kinds of propaganda directives that the Communist Party's Propaganda Department issues to media outlets throughout China, where there will be certain items that one day will be permitted and the next day will not be permitted.

So whatever the specific timeline of events that happened in the mid- to late 1990s surrounding Falun Gong or some of the other Christian groups that Mr. Shan mentioned, overall, one way of thinking about the situation is that Party leaders were able to ban these groups because: (A) they could, and there was no institutional mechanism like an independent judiciary to stop them from being able to do that; and (B) because the Communist Party generally is very reluctant to tolerate groups or individuals who place any authority, spiritual or otherwise, above their allegiance to the Party.

Sometimes people use the term "political" to differentiate between incidents that trip the Party's wire or not. But I personally find this idea of whether one is giving allegiance to the Party first or is willing to make changes based on the Party's demands to be more helpful in terms of thinking about what really touches the nerves of the Communist Party.

So for Tibetans, it is the authority of the Dalai Lama. For persecuted human rights lawyers like Gao Zhisheng, it's the authority of the law and the idea of placing the authority of the law above the authority of the Party. For Falun Gong practitioners, it is a dedication to teachings centered on truthfulness, compassion, and tolerance, and the idea that these are the primary principles that one should follow in day-to-day life, rather than perhaps something that the Communist Party may or may not tell one to do.

To me, one of the crucial elements that helps to understand this dynamic is this idea of "transformation" that Ethan Gutmann mentioned. Whether it is Falun Gong practitioners, or in some cases people like Gao Zhisheng and others, this very real focus on transformation and on reeducation, which means that people are not necessarily being arrested because they're organizing politically or organizing into some kind of group. Rather, certainly in the more spiritual cases, the efforts by the authorities are to get these people to change how they think.

It is very Orwellian, when you talk to practitioners and others who have been persecuted in this way. It is very much like the Party is torturing you to get you to say 2+2=5. If you keep saying 2+2=4, even if you know 2+2=4, then that in itself can create a conflict and is one of the things that the Chinese Communist Party finds threatening.

I just thought that might be another angle that could be helpful for thinking about these kinds of questions. In terms of some of the findings that Freedom House reports have indicated over the past 10 years, I went through many of the reports and I am just going to talk about a few of the aspects, and then I'll turn a little bit more in detail to Gao Zhisheng's story.

First, is this issue of large-scale detentions and widespread surveillance. According to our findings, perhaps after a lull because there was such an intense level of detentions and surveillance in the early years of the persecution, in the last couple of years, with the run-up to the Olympics and with a series of politically sensitive anniversaries, and as part of a much broader crackdown and intensification of the Communist Party's efforts to control Chinese society, we saw an intensification of the pressure on Falun Gong practitioners. There is a range of abuses, though. Some are arrested and some are not. Some are put under surveillance. But we certainly saw an intensification of those efforts targeting that group.

Second, is ongoing torture and deaths in custody. At Freedom House, we do not have the resources to maintain a comprehensive record of these deaths, but every year there are several well-documented cases of Falun Gong practitioners who are picked up and then killed in custody. There was one Beijing musician, in early

2008, who was stopped by police with his wife and the officers found Falun Gong literature in their car and the two were detained. He died in custody 11 days later. He was in his early forties. His wife was subsequently sentenced to three years in prison.

So there are cases like that, and as Ethan had mentioned, there are overseas Falun Gong groups who have collected pretty detailed accounts, even though it has not been fully independently verified, of over 3,000 cases similar to this young man's.

The third thing that we've observed is the sentencing of practitioners to long prison terms following unfair trials or to reeducation through labor camps by bureaucratic fiat. I would tend to agree with Ethan's efforts to try to understand what the real number is of people who are detained in these camps.

There was a fascinating study by the Chinese Human Rights Defenders group, if anyone would like to look it up, from February 2009, where they went and spoke to petitioners who had recently been released from labor camps and interviewed them. Many of these people said that, in addition to the petty thieves and drug addicts who make up many of the people in the reeducation through labor camps, Falun Gong practitioners constituted a significant percentage of the people in those camps and there were quite a large number of Christians in some of those facilities as well.

Some of the conversations I have personally had with people who came out of these camps included their talking about 140 religious prisoners, mostly Falun Gong practitioners, sometimes several hundred within an individual camp. So when you look at the nationwide labor camp population and you start to do the math, thinking about how many hundreds of camps there are in China, the number gets up very high, into the tens of thousands, quite quickly.

The last thing, as I mentioned earlier, is that I do quite a bit of research on Chinese media and the Internet. Clearly, Falun Gong is one of the permanent taboo topics and really one of the most systematically censored on the Chinese Internet. But what you also see happening is that people who try to spread information anyway end up getting imprisoned and they could be Falun Gong practitioners or non-Falun Gong practitioners. There was a recent case of a Chinese democracy activist who was sentenced to three years in prison because he had been caught with DVDs that had information related to Falun Gong on them.

So it is in the context of this kind of large-scale persecution of religious minorities that Gao Zhisheng and some of the other lawyers who have sought to represent Falun Gong practitioners come into the picture. Just a little bit of brief background on Gao: He was born in rural Shaanxi Province, where there are these cave dwellings, and that's where he grew up.

In the late 1980s, he was selling vegetables on the streets of Xinjiang Province and saw an advertisement that China wanted to train more lawyers. So, with just a middle-school education, he taught himself law, and in 1995, he passed the bar exam. Almost immediately he started taking pro bono cases for the full gamut of vulnerable groups, from coal miners, to workers. He very quickly became known nationwide and was actually named by the Ministry of Justice itself as one of the Top 10 Lawyers in China in 2001.

So it was in this context that, in 2004, Falun Gong practitioners started approaching him to see if this lawyer could help them, and he was hired by an adherent who had been sentenced to a labor camp. He tried to file for judicial review, to have that person's case reviewed, because the man had done nothing wrong, other than being known as a Falun Gong practitioner.

He went to the judges and the judges would not even look at the case. They would say, "Don't you know we don't take Falun Gong cases?" So what he decided to do as recourse was to write a letter to the National People's Congress. But the incident also sparked his interest in doing a more systematic investigation into what was happening to this group. It was as a result of those investigations that, in October and December 2005, he wrote the two open letters to Hu Jintao and Wen Jiabao that Doug mentioned earlier.

As Doug mentioned, in response, he and his family have been put under increasing pressure and abuse themselves. I will not go through all of the details of the last few years since Doug had spoken about it, but he disappeared several times and was held in incommunicado detention. It was really only in early February 2009, in an incredible feat of courage, that we learned the full details of the torture he had suffered during one of his previous detentions.

He issued a letter that was published overseas after he managed to sneak it out. In it, he chronicles being stripped naked and shocked with electric batons on his genitals, among other acts of torture. The guards, at least the way he describes it, told him that the conclusions of his investigations into what had happened to Falun Gong practitioners were indeed accurate, and in fact, the very torture methods they were using on him were ones that had been "perfected" on Falun Gong practitioners previously.

Similar to this point of "transformation" that I was talking about, they continuously tried to pressure him that if he would simply write some kind of article attacking Falun Gong, denouncing the previous letters he had written and praising the Party, then the torture would cease.

Eventually he was released, but almost immediately with the release and publication of this letter he was abducted again. His family fled to Thailand from China and is now in New York, but he has remained disappeared throughout most of 2009. Many of his friends, colleagues, and lawyers thought he had actually been killed in prison. He resurfaced in March 2010, and then disappeared again in April 2010.

Ironically, Gao actually never got a chance to represent a Falun Gong practitioner in court, but there are over 20 lawyers who have followed his lead—and he really broke open this taboo—and have done so.

In response, they have also faced temporary or permanent disbarment or being beaten. In at least one case, a lawyer, Wang Yonghang, was imprisoned for seven years under the same legal provision—that is, this vague legal provision—used to justify the imprisonment of his Falun Gong clients.

The treatment of these lawyers raises two broader points related to the future of religious freedom, but also the future of the rule of law. First, what you see very clearly is that the tactics that are used and developed to suppress one group can be quickly applied to others. From the vague legal provisions, to "black jails," to torture and transformation methods, we have seen these spreading.

In fact, when you speak to the lawyers and you ask them why they are taking on these super-sensitive cases that are clearly putting them and their families at tremendous risk, it is because, at least the way they explain it, that they feel very strongly that if this can happen to a group like Falun Gong practitioners then it can happen to anyone. Especially, since many of them are Christians, they feel that it could also happen to Christians and that the only way to protect believers is to create the kind of independent institutions and rule of law that will protect citizens from the Party's arbitrary actions.

Second, I think the more depressing side of it is that the Communist Party's very intransigent and harsh response to these lawyers really points to the limitations for progress toward the rule of law under the current Communist Party leadership. According to experts like Jerome Cohen, even reforms that had taken place in previous years have been backsliding.

The point I want to conclude with is actually optimistic, believe it or not, because parallel to this increased repression that we've seen is also a growing rights consciousness among ordinary citizens. In fact, you could argue that the increasing insecurity of the regime and its increased repression is in response to this growing and more assertive Chinese citizenry. Along with workers, bloggers, and journalists, Falun Gong practitioners are also those, as Ethan mentioned, who have used incredible ingenuity and creativity to challenge the repression against them.

So I am just going to end with one last quotation from Gao, where he reflects, in terms of his own observations, on the effects that some of these actions, whether it is through the Internet or other types of grassroots efforts to talk to the Chinese people and try to convince them to change how they think about Falun Gong.

> More and more people around me, including professional scholars, government staff members, and ordinary Chinese citizens have begun to question the rationale behind the campaign against these believers. This has been a palpable change. These people have come to realize how unjust, inhumane, and lawless the government's violent persecution of the Falun Gong people is. This rapid, widespread change in attitude stands in stark contrast to the government's static, outdated practices.

Now, if you talk to a lot of Chinese people, largely because of the media censorship and fears of repercussion, you can get all kinds of answers related to what they think about Falun Gong. But it's still quite interesting to hear from somebody like Gao Zhisheng, who is tapped into the grassroots level of society that at least with some of the people in the circles that he was interacting with, there had been a change in how they were thinking about this group.

So, I just wanted to say thank you, and to end on the last thought that I really do hope that at some point Gao Zhisheng will be able to be here himself to share with you what he has to say.

[The prepared statement of Ms. Cook appears in the appendix.]

Mr. GROB. Thank you very much, Sarah.

Thank you to all four of our panelists for some outstanding presentations.

I would like to open the floor up, for the time remaining, for questions.

Ms. FORD. I submitted written testimony for the record and it's outside. But going to this basic question raised by the panel, of how do we understand the causes of the suppression in China and what are some of the prospects for reconciliation between Falun Gong and the Communist Party. In order to understand those questions, it's valuable to look back at 1999 and really try to understand what the social dynamics were that led to the ban on Falun Gong.

Mr. GROB. Would you stand, please, and turn around?

Ms. FORD. You've heard a few different explanations for why Falun Gong was initially targeted, and those include peaceful demonstration at Zhongnanhai in April 1999, which as Ethan has alluded to, may have been something of a bait and switch. We also heard about sort of institutional reasons; Falun Gong is a large, independent civil society organization, and in China you simply don't have large, independent civil society organizations—let alone spiritual or religious groups. There's also the size of Falun Gong, a few million on the very low end, up to, by some estimates, 70 to 100 million at the high end. This represents an enormous number of people who are operating outside of official sanction.

I could go on. Scholars have posited a number of other explanations in the broader historical context. But in my view, I think you need to look at the nature of the Party itself. The Party is essentially a theocracy. It's a theocracy, except that it's purely a secular one. But it's essentially a religion. The fact that people don't believe in the Marxist religion doesn't make that any less so, it just means that the appeal of the theology is more tenuous. And so the Falun Gong, not deliberately but just by its mere existence and its spiritual orientation, poses a challenge to that. Falun Gong is associated with the Buddhist school of thought, so it implicitly challenges the atheism of the party.

Falun Gong, for instance, holds a belief in divine authority, where Marxism believes in human agency. Falun Gong teaches that morality, compassion, and virtue are measures of progress and value, where the Communist Party believes in material progress. When Falun Gong was first banned in 1999, the official editorials from the state-run press actually posited that this was the cause of the ban; they put forth a dichotomy between theism and atheism, and suggested that Falun Gong's spirituality and emphasis on virtue and the divine was incompatible with the official ideology. I think probably the most candid statement came from an editorial in Xinhua on July 27, 1999, which said simply that the truth, compassion, and tolerance principles preached by the Falun Gong have nothing in common with the Socialist ethic and cultural progress we are trying to achieve. There are more of these kinds of remarks in my written testimony. But I think this underlies the fact that Falun Gong is not a legitimate threat, it's not political, and it's certainly never sought to be a political threat to the ruling party. What the Communist Party fears is people who derive moral authority from something other than itself.

So I think this sort of understanding is just useful in evaluating, what are the prospects of reconciliation, what are the prospects for ending the persecution. I'll stop there because I know that we're somewhat over time. So, thanks for the opportunity to share that.

Mr. GROB. Thank you very much for those remarks.

Yes, please. Mr. Geheran?

Mr. GEHERAN. Hi. I'm Jim Geheran with Intiatives for China. Thank you. This is a most wonderful panel here. What I'm hearing is that it's the very nature of the Chinese Government that they see anything that poses principles or an organization that is hedging on their power is a threat and is fair game to be stamped out. So the conclusion that I'm hearing is that the Government of China, despite its claims of harmony and stability, has succeeded in alienating just about every segment of Chinese society, whether it's religious, labor, or whatever.

My question to you, if anyone cares to comment on it, is: Where is all this alienation going? Where is this frustration being parked if so much of the Chinese population is being alienated, and what are the consequences for stability that the apparent policy of the American Government is just to look the other way? Are we setting ourselves up for another revolution?

Mr. GROB. Thank you very much.

Professor Tong, would you like to comment?

Mr. TONG. I think this is an important political agenda among the Party leadership. I don't think anyone knows the answer. They don't have any solution to it. The way they try to handle the problem is to manage the problem and not to eradicate it. They try to localize it so that either labor movements or discharged PLA soldiers or persons would not form cross-county, cross-city, or cross-province coalitions. That is, I think, the best that they can do. So, I will leave it at that.

Mr. GROB. Thank you very much.

Other questions? Yes, sir?

AUDIENCE PARTICIPANT. [Inaudible]—from Human Rights—I have a question about the——[inaudible].

Mr. GROB. Thank you for those remarks.

Any other questions, comments from the audience?

AUDIENCE PARTICIPANT. A question for Mr. Gutmann. [Inaudible.]

Mr. GUTMANN. I certainly take James Tong's point that there is, over time, less official Chinese recognition of Falun Gong as a problem. I think that has some basis. I mean, if I were saying that there were a million in detention in 2004, it might well be half a million now.

But last I checked—and I was still doing interviews on this in 2008, interviewing people who were fresh out of labor camp, fresh out of the *laogai* —they were not reporting any kind of decrease in the prison population, the *laogai* system population overall. Now, you might say, well, these are refugees, and so on. Maybe, but I wasn't pushing them for that answer.

I'm asking them the same questions. I'm going round the question a different way, but I'm coming back to the same point: How many of your people were in your cell block? How many other kinds of people were in your cell block? It might take a day before I'd even approach that question, just to get to the point where they were relaxed enough to just answer it casually, which is what I'm after. And from those responses, I do not sense a major decrease in Falun Gong populations.

I think your point is well taken. Falun Gong has pointed to the Beijing roundups, the Shanghai roundups before the Olympics and other events—events that get a lot of press. But frankly, most of the prisoners are coming out of the provinces. They're not coming out of Shanghai and Beijing. That's where the big numbers are, and those numbers are fairly unchanging.

Mr. GROB. Thank you very much.

Other questions? Yes, in the back.

AUDIENCE PARTICIPANT. [Inaudible.]

Mr. GROB. Professor Tong, then Mr. Shan.

Mr. TONG. Indeed, that is happening. So Mr. Grob earlier made reference to the rule of law. You cannot have rule of law that would promulgate specific and arbitrary legislation, for manufacturers and consumers, or for individual entrepreneurs and for foreign investors, but denying it to the religious communities—you cannot protect the economic interests and assets of the accountholders of the Shanghai and Shenzhen Stock Exchanges, but denying it to religious groups, and not protecting their economic interests.

Now religious personnel can collect fees for performing religious functions. Religious organizations can collect donations from both individuals and corporations both domestically and also internationally. One of the reasons is that if they allow non-government organizations like those in Legal Aid, women's groups, the disabled, and environmental protection, to receive gifts, both from individuals and corporations, both domestically as well as from international organizations, they cannot deny religious communities from receiving it.

This is also what is happening. The rule of law cannot discriminate. This is what is happening to the religious communities as well. This is why I say that the religious policy is the collateral beneficiary of market reforms. So today, in the past 10 years, every year, there were over 100 Protestant and Roman Catholic priests, nuns, and seminarians that are in the United States. Right now there are 300 Roman Catholic priests and seminarians in the Philippines alone. There are Roman Catholic priests that serve as chaplains in top universities in China. There are Roman Catholic priests teaching philosophy in top universities in China. There is a Roman Catholic priest, a foreigner, who serves as the director of a leprosy sanitarium in China. In these areas, China has relaxed its religious policy.

Even for the five official religions—the State Administration of Religious Affairs has established a sixth division. It used to be just the five divisions each for an official religion. They have established a sixth division for the other unofficial religions. In some provinces the Eastern Orthodox religion is now an official religion. In some provinces, some folk religions are also officially recognized.

Mr. GROB. Thank you, Professor Tong.

Mr. Shan, would you like to add?

Mr. SHAN. Yes. I think the Chinese Government is open to economics. They have developed a strong national capitalist system which is different from Western capitalism. As that lady mentioned, when we talk about, is it possible that the Chinese can give much more room to religion as economics; first we need to consider the feature of the government, the Communist system.

So, I mean, the Chinese Government, the open market for economics; it's basically something that's not new. Before the Communist Party took over China, in all of China's history, China has been a free market country, or nation. But yet, every Chinese Government is sensitive to any religions or spiritual movements who touch politics. "Touch politics" means trying to use spiritual or religious ideas to justify or to deny the rulings of the government.

So though they even allow some freedom through a series of religious systems and policies, they are still very careful with those religions, especially toward religion called monotheist religions: Islam, Christianity, and Catholicism. These monotheist religions are really powerful. They have played important roles in the whole world's history, so the Chinese Government knows that, even without the lessons from Eastern Europe. The Chinese Government and the Communist Party will continue to suppress or restrict those religions.

Mr. GROB. Thank you.

Ms. Cook?

Ms. COOK. The term that Professor Tong used about managing is really very relevant, because what you see the Communist Party doing, is that there is this divide-and-conquer strategy, this fragmentation of issues, and this idea that in order to maintain overall control you don't necessarily have to control everything. So what you can see is that maybe certain groups will be allowed to be in this legal gray zone, while other groups will be subjected to horrific and systematic campaigns.

I think my underlying point was that you have a dynamic that is arbitrary, and that can change at any time. In my personal opinion, looking at some of the dynamics related to the house church movement now, there are some worrying signs—I obviously very much hope it does not go in the direction of what has happened to Falun Gong practitioners—but there are a lot of similarities to what the dynamics were surrounding Falun Gong in the late 1990s, even just in terms of the sheer number of believers.

Also, it is interesting, this question of whether people view themselves as political, because whether you talk to Falun Gong practitioners or you talk to petitioners who are trying to protest some kind of injustice, they often, at least initially, wouldn't necessarily see their actions as being political.

They see their appeals as being an effort to address some kind of grievance that they've encountered personally. In the case of Falun Gong practitioners, there was the appeal on April 25—and Ethan can talk about this, if we have a moment for him to talk about his version of events. Or, if you have a chance to read his article, it really is fascinating in terms of the description of his account of what happened on April 25.

Falun Gong practitioners weren't necessarily there to ask for an overthrow of the Chinese Government. They were there because they wanted to try to register as a group, because they previously tried to register repeatedly and weren't allowed; they were there to ask for the release of people who had been arrested, as Ethan described, in Tianjin; and they were there to ask that the books of their spiritual teachings that had been banned be allowed to be published again. That's very similar to the requests you see petitioners coming to Beijing over—because they've been evicted from their home, or their child died in the earthquake in Sichuan Province and they want some kind of compensation.

So it's interesting because you see this process that a lot of individuals are going through, where it starts like that, where they just have a grievance that relates to something in their personal life that they don't at all think of as political, but as they start to encounter the system and encounter the intolerance of the system vis-a-vis their efforts to find justice for this grievance, that's when you see people starting to question the authority of the Party.

If you talk to Falun Gong practitioners now, they'll still say, "Oh, no, we're not political." They'll explain it in the sense that "We don't want any political power, we don't want to replace the Communist Party." But there is a sense that so long as the Communist Party is in power it's going to be very difficult for Falun Gong practitioners to have full freedom of religion. There are real difficulties there in terms of what you might do upon coming to that conclusion.

I think the only other quick point I wanted to make is that there is also an economic dimension to the persecution. That relates to the incentive systems, where you see, even at very low levels, notices on official Web sites offering rewards to members of the public who will turn in a Falun Gong practitioner who they notice putting up a posting.

This defector Ethan mentioned who had come from the 6–10 Office and whose media interviews I've read talks about rewards for people who transform Falun Gong practitioners. Other evidence points to quotas for the number of transformed Falun Gong practitioners and promotions being determined based on that.

So one of the things that you see is that these incentive systems almost take on a life of their own. That's clearly an element in some of these issues related to organ transplants, in terms of the creation of a market and the incentives that that creates.

That economic dimension is something to think about. It's something you see in other areas of Chinese society in terms of the way the Communist Party manages its control. You see that with censorship, as a certain commercialization of censorship where the risk that newspapers face, that Internet companies face if they transgress political directives that are handed down by the Party are not just political punishments. It is not just that you're going to be fired, it's that your business could be shut down and that there are very real economic implications to that.

So one ends up with these economic incentives that actually drive some of the political repression that we're seeing, and that's part of the sophistication and the difference, perhaps, between the China that we see today and the Soviet Union during the Cold War. So, I'll just end there. I know that was a bit of a long comment, but I hope that's helpful.

Mr. GROB. Thank you very much, Sarah.

Ethan, did you want to jump in?

Mr. GUTMANN. Just very briefly. Minister X—I can't give his name—was a financial minister at the provincial level and he described Party meetings in 1998 and early 1999. The explanation given for eliminating Falun Gong was really simple. It was just that Jiang Zemin had a problem. Tiananmen Square would not go away. It interfered with his legitimacy. They had to have a new target. It was that simple.

I'm not saying that's the ultimate explanation and I'm not saying it's a perfect explanation, but inside the Party, that was the explanation. One of the tensions you feel on this panel about the overall subject is this: Is the Falun Gong crackdown indicative of how China is handling religious affairs? It's not clear. There are some ambiguities there. The Falun Gong crackdown, in some ways, can be seen as a stand-alone.

Yet I hate to use Chinese proverbs here, but you kill the chicken to scare the monkey, or if you like, a Western proverb from the New York Review of Books—the anaconda in the chandelier. The proverbs mean much the same thing, which is that they are setting an example. They are making it very clear that there are parameters. And you don't know when the anaconda is going to come down, and you don't know when the chicken is going to be slaughtered. That condition applies to religious believers and it applies to just about every other group in China as well.

Mr. GROB. Thank you very much. We are over time. That was somewhat discretionary on my part. The problem with having four eloquent and knowledgeable panelists together with a collection of eloquent and knowledgeable members of the audience, is it makes my job as time-keeping taskmaster much more difficult.

So I'd like to wrap it up and just ask one last time if any of our panelists have a 15-second final thought that they would like to add.

Ms. COOK. I do.

Mr. GROB. Please.

Ms. COOK. I thought somebody in the audience might ask the question, well, what do we do about this? So I was trying to think about what might be some of the recommendations I could offer. I think there are a few things that might be worth keeping in mind, though these maybe touch a little bit more on the micro level than the macro level.

One recommendation relates to international attention to individual cases and the difference that it makes. Really, Gao Zhisheng would not be alive, and there are many other former prisoners of conscience that I have spoken to who would not be alive today, if it had not been for the international attention to their cases. As badly as Gao was treated, I think they would have treated him even worse if they knew that they could just make him disappear and no one would ask any questions.

Of course, that is the problem for some of the anonymous Falun Gong practitioners who may have had their organs harvested. So, I think that's one thing to just keep in mind, that the advocacy for individual cases really makes a difference.

Another thing in terms of perhaps U.S. Government policy is that one of the real difficulties when dealing with an issue like this—and it's amazing to be able to get a panel like this to take place—but this really is a topic that, because of the sensitivity of the Communist Party, there's very little good research on it. It's something we encounter in doing our research. So, my recommendation would be to try to find a way to fund really detailed assessments of individual cases. So how do you verify individual cases?

In some ways, the lawyers can be a channel for that because you can find ways in which the lawyers can maybe anonymously be able to talk about what happened to their clients—who has actually been imprisoned, for how many years in a way that might be possible to verify or cross-reference with some of the reports coming from ChinaAid on Christians or from the Falun Dafa Information Center on Falun Gong.

The last thing I would say is just that the things also happen outside of China. I could talk a whole lot—I'm sure Ethan could, too, and others here as well—about the lengths the Communist Party goes to outside of China to try to censor conversations like the one we're having here, whether it's about this topic or it's about the Uyghurs, or it's about Tibetans, or it's about any other topic that the Communist Party finds sensitive. It's amazing how many incidents there are of events that have been planned and at the last minute get called off. So from that perspective, I really do commend the CECC for holding this panel.

So, for anybody who engages in these kinds of issues or comes across this, one of the experiences I have seen is that you can call the Communist Party's bluff. So when that call comes from the Chinese official saying, "Oh, you know, don't hold this event," then you can call their bluff. There also have been cases where such incidents went to court, and courts in Israel and Taiwan ruled that Falun Gong practitioners should be able to exercise their right to free expression.

So I'll just end on that note. Maybe other people on the panel have thoughts, but I felt this would perhaps be a slightly more optimistic way of ending the discussion. That way, we're not just thinking in terms of "Oh, my gosh, look at these terrible things that are happening in China," but also in terms of what we can do about it sitting over here.

Mr. GROB. Thank you very much.

Any others?

Mr. GUTMANN. Since Copenhagen, the Obama Administration has done pretty close to a 180-degree turn on China. The State Department is seriously considering giving the Global Internet Freedom Consortium money. We don't know if the press reports are totally accurate, but this is very significant, a big change. Frankly, I believe that for all these causes, but particularly for religious causes—and I'm not just talking about Falun Gong here—a free Internet is essential.

If my small voice can make any difference in encouraging this development, hopefully it'll move through. We really are seeing a concerted effort to overcome the Big Brother Internet—not just temporarily, not just in China, but as a template for the world.

Mr. GROB. Thank you very much, Ethan.

Professor Tong?

Mr. TONG. This year is the 500th anniversary of the death of Mateo Ricci, one of the first Roman Catholic missionaries who entered China. I think the lesson from all of this is this: for spiritual religious movements that want to spread and grow inside China, one should think about strategy. Then, in the Catholic church, the question they were faced with was whether they would insist on doctrinal purity, that is, outside the church no salvation, and also ancestral worship in China as well, because the Roman Catholic church forbade it.

But for Ricci and fellow missionaries, this was less of an issue as finding the right strategy. There are certain things that need to be emphasized, there are certain things that need not. It could also be the case that you are wrong, your doctrine could be wrong. So for Ricci, who waited 16 years just to find an audience with the Chinese Emperor, he waited. He did not insist on these doctrines. Finally, many colleagues of his Jesuit order found employment in the court. So the question is, one needs to find common ground and what is possible and what is not possible under the existing circumstances in China. That is, I think, worth considering.

Mr. GROB. Thank you very much, Professor Tong.

Mr. Shan, would you like to have the last word?

Mr. SHAN. Yes. Thank you. I think, related to Sarah's comment, what should we do to improve the situation of religious freedom in China, I think of course we should be optimistic in our wish and desires, but I would think that we should have a practical method or agenda to do that. We will say, okay, once China becomes a democratic country, it will solve the problems. That is true. But actually, from a sociology perspective, we know in Western countries, especially in Europe, how democracies came out. It was based on the citizen country built first, which means that citizenship should be first founded and established in a country according to law, then the next step would be democracy.

So China is still not a real citizen society. But if you become a citizen society first, even without democracy, religious freedom, except political freedom, will be improved, like Taiwan, before their democracy, and Singapore was a dictatorship country, but they all allow religious freedom because they are a citizen society. A citizen society feature would be fourfold: you have civil rights, social rights, political rights, and religious rights. So I think that's something we should put effort in for the first step.

Mr. GROB. Well, thank you very much.

This month marks the 47th anniversary of the famous civil rights address by President Kennedy in which he quite notably said that, "The rights of every man are diminished when the rights of one man are threatened." It is in that spirit that we address this issue.

The entire transcript of this proceeding, including statements submitted by our panelists for the record, and the discussion here today will be published and available online through our Web site and in hard copy. We look forward to the continuation of this discussion on this important topic.

With that, thank you to our panelists. Thank you in the audience. This roundtable is adjourned. [Applause.]

[Whereupon, at 3:58 p.m. the roundtable was adjourned.]

APPENDIX

PREPARED STATEMENTS

PREPARED STATEMENT OF JAMES TONG

JUNE 18, 2010

Thanks you for inviting me to participate in this roundtable. My remarks will focus on three issues. The first is how the Chinese Government views the level of political and security threat the Falun Gong presents in recent years. The second is what type of Falun Gong practitioners and their activities the Chinese Government considered illegal and unacceptable, and ground for legal sanction. The third are the implications for the Chinese Government positions on religious freedom at large.

I. THE DIMINISHED SECURITY THREAT OF THE FALUN GONG IN CHINA

Last July was the 10th anniversary of the banning of the Falun Gong in China. In the past decade, the Chinese state has been effective in suppressing the public forms of the organized activities of the Falun Gong. Before the imposition of the ban on July 22, 1999, there were between 2.3 to 80 million practitioners of the Falun Gong. They were organized into 39 main stations, 1,900 guidance stations, and 28,000 practice sites. Every morning, these assemblies of Falun Gong practitioners conducted breathing exercises in city parks and town squares. They also gathered in special convocations in sports arenas and auditoriums on special anniversaries. There were also training sessions lasting 3–4 days where practitioners learnt more advanced breathing exercise, meditation techniques and Falun Gong doctrine. Since July 22, 1999, these three forms of organized activities (morning assemblies, large convocations, training seminars) can no longer be seen in public. All known Falun Gong organizations (main stations, guidance stations, practice sites) are duly registered and the assemblies disbanded. Their leaders were arrested, went into hiding or self-exile. The rank and file practitioners were registered, and required to write severance papers where they declared their official withdrawal from the Falun Gong. Its publications met a similar fate. Before the official ban, the Falun Gong published 11 titles. Total distribution of these publications by the Beijing head office (Falun Dafa Research Society) was over 11 million copies. As part of the ban, all copies of these Falun Gong publications were seized, their existing stock confiscated. On the 7th day of the ban (July 29), mass rallies were held in 17 major cities where these publications were set ablaze or turned into paper pulp. In sum, these organized activities of the Falun Gong, as well as their publications enterprise, did not outlive the official ban on the Falun Gong imposed on July 22, 1999.

There are still periodic reports in official media on arrests of Falun Gong practitioners for staging protests in provincial and national capitals, sabotaging media broadcasts, displaying Falungong banners in public places, but these acts of overt defiance have become rare in recent years. These can be seen in three developments. The first is the annual report of the Chief Procurator (the equivalent of the Attorney-General), which enumerates the major law-enforcement problems in China in the given year. From 1999–2003, the Falun Gong was listed as a major law-enforcement problem nation-wide. But from 2004 on, it was dropped from the list. Below the national level, each of the 31 provinces also issues its annual procuracy report, and these largely mirror the national trend. From 1999 to 2001, a great majority of the 31 provinces (29 in 1999, 28 in 2000, 21 in 2001) list the Falun Gong as a major law-enforcement problem in their province. But from 2004 to 2008, there was a monotonic decline from 7 in 2004 to 2 in 2008.

The second related development is the absence of followup campaigns to consolidate the gains of the crackdown and to mop up Falun Gong remnants and resurgent elements. After the initial nationwide blitzkrieg in late July, 1999, a four-month nation-wide Strike at the Falun Gong campaign was launched in summer, 2001, to ferret out fugitive Falun Gong leaders, underground Falun Gong hide-outs, inventories of Falun Gong publications they had missed in the first security-round-up. For some Falun Gong strongholds, local law-enforcement agencies conducted single-day campaigns every quarter, or on Falun Gong special occasions. Other localities organized sustained 100-day campaigns to systematically check all printing shops, photocopying vendors, Internet cafes and rental properties for suspicious Falun Gong activities. From 2003–2008, no such followup campaign aimed at crushing the Falun Gong has been reported.

The third related development was the re-reorganization of the special law-enforcement agency that deals with the Falun Gong. To prepare for the crackdown, a special agency called the "June 10" Office was established at both the central, provincial, and municipal levels, and even within universities and large state-owned enterprises, with the exclusive mission to organize, manage and coordinate the business of arresting, registering, detaining, interrogating Falun Gong practitioners, and dissolving Falun Gong organizations. As the name suggests, most were established on June 10, or 40 days before the crackdown on July 22, 1999. Their full office titles were "the Office dealing with the Falun Gong" or the "Office dealing with the problem of Cults." After April 2002, close to three years after the crackdown, most of these offices were renamed "Offices to maintain social stability." Their mission was broadened to encompass other serious sources of social stability in the locality, including the protests of laid-off workers, those who have lost their pensions, peasants evicted from their land by real-estate developers, tenants with disputes against landlords in housing projects. In combination, such absence of followup campaigns, the lack of reference to the Falun Gong as a local serious security problem in national and provincial procuracy reports, the reorganization of the June Offices to deal with other local security issues, suggest that the Falun Gong has ceased to be a serious political threat and security problem for the regime since 2003 or 2004 to 2008, both at the national and provincial levels.

II. DIFFERENTIATION OF OFFENCES BY AND SANCTIONS OF FALUN GONG PRACTITIONERS

Next, I want to address the question of what type of Falun Gong practitioners and what type of offences warranted regime sanction. Let me begin with the simple fact that there was wide-ranging estimates of the number of Falun Gong practitioners in July 1999 before the official crackdown. The estimate varies because there is no clear definition of what is a Falun Gong practitioner. Unlike Christians, there is no rite of formal induction into the religious community. Falun Gong organizations also did not keep a roster of its practitioners. Even at the conservative low-end estimate of 2.3 million, mass detention and incarceration of Falun Gong practitioners was out of the question. 2.3 million is 4 times the total population of Washington DC. Even for an authoritarian state, the Chinese judicial system lacked the capacity to process 2.3 million cases. There were not enough judges and prosecutors to prosecute, indict, convict and sentence 2.3 million cases, public security agents to enforce coercive detention, and the prison and labor reform systems to house them. In 1998, the year before the crackdown, the total number of criminal cases prosecuted in Chinese courts was 400,000, and total number of defendants was under 600,000. These include all cases—homicide, assault, robbery, fraud. At that rate, it would take the Chinese courts at least 4 years to process the 2.3 million cases. If we use the smaller number of only cases pertaining to endangering state security, endangering social order, obstructing social order (the usual alleged crimes that Falun Gong practitioners were charged), the Chinese court system in 1998 processed under 74,000 cases of such offences. At that rate, it would take them 31 years to clear the 2.3 million cases. Clearly, lacking the capacity to process all these cases, they need to differentiate among Falun Gong practitioners.

On the same official notice announcing the ban issued on July 22, 1999, Falun Gong practitioners were divided into four types. For the great majority, rank and file members, there would be no disciplinary action taken, provided they would sign a document renouncing the Falun Gong and withdrawing from the congregation, after which their names would be entered into a registry. Disciplinary action refers to dismissal or demotion from positions held in government agencies or enterprises, denial or reduction of staff benefits, expulsion from the Chinese Communist Party, and prosecution in case of alleged criminal offences. The triage applies to three types of core leaders. The first group were those who had participated in illegal activities—participating in protest rallies and distributing Falun Gong publications on the official black list. If they would also renounce and withdraw from the Falun Gong, and provide an account of these activities, then no disciplinary action would be taken. The second type of core leaders were those who had committed serious errors, not only participating in, but facilitating protest rallies, not only distributing, but printing Falun Gong publications. If they would also renounce, withdraw from the Falun Gong, account for their activities, and in addition, provide a conscientious confession and self-examination, and accrue merit (persuading other practitioners to confess, informing authorities where the hide-outs were, finger-pointing other core leaders), then no disciplinary action would be taken. The third type is where the sanctions and disciplinary actions would be imposed. These were the core leaders who planned and organized "political turmoil," viz, protest rallies in front of party and government headquarters and other public places without permission, and who remained unrepentant (refusing to renounce or withdraw from the Falun Gong, not providing information about the Falun Gong activities and leaders), then they would be dismissed from the Party, or government post, sent to labor reform institutions, or prosecuted in trial if criminal laws were violated.

III. IMPLICATIONS FOR RELIGIOUS FREEDOM IN CHINA

The foregoing analysis suggests several implications for the larger issue of religious freedom in China. The first is religion is still a managed religion in China. The state claims the right to manage religion. It claims the authority to define what is religion and what is a cult, what is official religion and what is not official religion, what is normal religious activities and what are not. There are religious affairs bureau at the national, provincial, municipal, and at county levels in China. The state requires the mandatory registration of all religious organizations and religious venues, and approval of the publishing and distribution of the Christian Bible.

Second, the capacity of the party-state to manage religion has been eroded by market economy. On the supply side, the market economy has created political space where heterodox spiritual movements can survive outside the control of the party-state. In the Maoist planned economy, where virtually the entire working population were employed in government owned enterprises, lived in public housing, relied on government issued ration-coupons to get their daily necessities, religious believers who defied state rule could find no job, no housing, no food, no clothing. With the establishment of private and foreign owned enterprises, the end of rationing and the creation of the housing market, religious believers do not have to choose between practicing their faith and their maintaining their livelihood.

On the demand side, 30 years of the market economy has fostered other social issues that pose threats to the social order and that compete for administrative attention and action. The annual procuracy report lists a rising crime wave, manifested in organized crime, murder, robbery, kidnapping, drug trafficking as serious law-enforcement problems. Aside from rising crime, the regime has to contend with another source of social instability. Market reform has created sources of social conflict that did not exist in the Maoist era—unemployed workers, those who lost their pensions because their companies went bankrupt, discharged soldiers who could not live on their meager severance pay, peasants evicted from their farms because the township secretary colluded with real-estate developer. In 1994, there were 10,000 of these collective protests with 50 or more participants. The number was increased to 74,000 in 2004, or more than 200 incidents per day. In May 2004 alone, there were 2,180 collective protests each with 500 or more participants. With demonstrators in the street or outside their offices, these are much more urgent problems that the regime had to take care of. In comparison to organized and violent crime, or collective protests, religious congregations are much more tame, and it is not in the interest of the regime to drive them to the street to join other demonstrators.

Third, a more benign religious policy is also the collateral beneficiary of market reforms. Before China launched its market reforms, there was convergence between its religious policy with the larger political, economic and social policies. China was a Communist state, subscribing to Communist ideology. Its 1973 Party Constitution states that the CCP is committed to the overthrow of capitalism and its replacement by the dictatorship of the proletariat. Its economic system was a centrally-planned, socialist economy, with no private ownership of means of production. There was no labor market and no capital market. In its social system, there was no civil society, no independent NGOs. Internationally, there was no foreign direct investments, nor foreign economic presence in China, and were few other links with the global community. There was a thus a close fit of its religious policy with other policies of a Leninist state—where the state had virtual total control over the economy and society, including religion. But with 30 years of market reform, there is increasing divergence between its religious policy with its political, economic and social policies. Politically, China has ceased to be a Communist state. Major Communist anniversaries, like the 150th anniversary of the publication of the Communist Manifesto, the 100th death anniversary of Karl Marx, the 90th anniversary of the Bolshevik Revolution, were not commemorated with a People's Daily editorial in post-reform China. In Orwellian fashion, the current version of the Party Constitution was changed to remove references to the overthrow of capitalism and the establishment of the dictatorship of the proletariat. Its economy is arguably a market economy, almost fully integrated with the global economy, with thriving labor and capital markets. There are now 150 million investment account holders in the Shanghai and Shenzhen Stock exchange, while there are only 72 million CCP members. One can say that there are twice as many capitalists as communists in China today. Socially, there is an emerging civil society, with over 200,000 registered social organizations, many are independent NGOs, some with international connections. There are thriving gay and lesbian communities in major cities, where open gay marriages are celebrated in downtown Beijing. Thus there is a increasing divergence between its political, economic and social policies with its religious policy, which is anachronistic, belonging the antiquated bygone Leninist era. Especially for a centralized, hierarchical system where first principles matter, China needs to reconcile its religious policy that is divergent with the more forward looking and progressive political, economic and social policies.

And in some important ways, it has. At least since the promulgation of the New Regulations on Religious Affairs of March 2005 if not earlier, the Chinese regime has granted increasing institutional autonomy to religious organizations and circumscribed the authority of the state to manage religion. Religious organizations are no longer required to accept the leadership of the CCP, to pledge support of socialism and patriotism, as some earlier religious regulations stipulated. The onerous requirement for mandatory, annual re-certification of religious venues was dropped. House fellowship Christians is allowed by a majority of provinces. The authority to certify religious personnel, to examine and admit candidates for religious schools, to determine the curriculum of seminaries, to appoint and dismiss prelates of religious venues, to set the number of religious personnel in religious venues and the number of religious venues in each locality, now rests with religious organizations and not with the local religious affairs bureaus. The economic interests of religious communities are protected. Religious personnel can collect fees for performing religious functions. Religious organizations can now receive donations from both individuals and corporations, and from both domestic and foreign individuals and institutions. They can also invest in income-generating property and collect rents. When religious property has to be relocated or demolished in eminent domain cases like highway constructions, they need to be compensated by fair market value that is independently appraised. In addition, religious organizations are not only permitted, but encouraged to engage in philanthropy and social welfare programs. Both the Protestant and Catholic churches now operate nursing homes, hundreds of clinics, plus mobile dental and ophthalmology units. The Catholic church has two leprosy sanatoriums. There are thriving YMCAs in major cities, offering athletic programs, vocation training courses, foreign language classes.

Just as significant, Chinese Christian churches have developed vital links with the global church. Many foreign religious leaders, including American evangelicals, superiors of Roman Catholic male religious orders have visited China multiple times, celebrated mass, gave retreats, and held conferences. Beyond visits, many faculty from Protestant and Catholic divinity schools in Europe, Canada and the United States have also taught in Protestant and Catholic seminaries in China. Outside seminaries, there are foreign Catholic priests who serve as a director of a leprosy sanatorium, chaplains in Chinese universities for American and European exchange students, professors with long-term contracts teaching philosophy and foreign languages in top Chinese universities. Conversely, hundreds of protestant and Catholic priests, nuns and seminaries have enrolled in degree programs in European, Canadian and U.S. divinity schools, after applying for and were granted exit visas and Chinese passports as religious personnel. One U.S. Catholic male religious order has sponsored over a hundred Chinese Catholic priests, nuns and seminarians to study in U.S. theologates. Upon completion of their European and North American divinity studies, some Chinese Christians now hold important positions in the church hierarchy. The present dean of the national Union Theological Protestant Seminary in Nanjing has a doctorate degree in divinity in Stockholm. The Seminary will have a new campus on 33 acres granted by the government, with a construction cost of 140 million yuan, some of it as grant or loan by the government.

To conclude, there is still no religious freedom in China of the kind as in the United States. The state still manages, monitors, and often intervenes in affairs of religious organizations. Outside the five official religions, the fate is worse. Unregistered temples and churches have been demolished, their property and publications confiscated, their prelates jailed. But compared to that of the Maoist era, or even of the past two decades, there has been conspicuous and substantial progress. Whether one views the degree of institutional autonomy of religious organizations, the protection of their economic interests, their ability to operate social welfare programs, and their freedom to foster links with their universal community, there are positive developments in all these fronts, some unprecedented in the history of the People's Republic. There are increasing signs that religious policy is converging with the political, economic, and social policies of the market reform era in China.

Thank you.

Prepared Statement of Ethan Gutmann

June 18, 2010

I want to thank the CECC, but my remarks need to go beyond the pro-forma on this point.

The Chinese Communist Party portrays Falun Gong as an evil cult and a terrorist entity. The Chinese State's diplomatic arm has made it clear that the Falun Gong issue is non-negotiable. It is relevant that this appears to be the first U.S. Government hearing or roundtable directly focusing on Falun Gong in a decade.

As a former Beijing business consultant, I do not rely on Chinese official statistics. For example, if you attempt to generate a population figure for the *laogai* system—labor camps, prisons, black jails, detention centers, and psychiatric hospitals—you get a figure well below a million. Yet if one counts every detention node and make common-sense estimates, as the Laogai Foundation researchers do every year, you get a more credible figure of 3 to 5 million.

According to the UN rapporteur on torture, Falun Gong comprises half of those prisoners, but this figure might be high. Much of my research is based on interviews with refugees and defectors. I don't ask them for estimates of the *laogai* system, but no matter how traumatized they are, I do expect them to remember how many Falun Gong were in their cell-block. After interviewing over 120 individuals, including defectors from inside Chinese security and well over 50 *laogai* refugees, I estimate that Falun Gong comprises between 15 to 20 percent of the *laogai* system. That's about half a million to a million Falun Gong in detention on average, representing the largest Chinese Security action since the Maoist period.

We often perceive Chinese human rights problems as an entrenched structure. But the Party's campaign against Falun Gong more closely resembles a blitzkrieg, in an increasingly global war, marked by physical assaults in the United States, Chinese operatives posing as refugees, and coordinated hacking of Chinese dissident networks and U.S. Government entities.

We should understand how the war began, the casualty rates, and the stakes of our neutrality. So I thank the CECC—and especially Toy Reid—for making this roundtable a reality.

I was in Beijing on July 20, 1999, when the official crackdown began and sound-trucks flooded the streets. Western reporters flooded the zone, but with little cooperation from either the Party or Falun Gong, journalists had trouble simply penciling in the first question of any news report: What is Falun Gong?

Falun Gong, simply put, is a Buddhist revival movement: moral passion, occasional talk of miracles, are-you-running-with-me-Master-Li individualism, and a reflexive mistrust of establishments and outsider agendas.

The Buddhist aspect may be unfamiliar and exotic, but, as Arthur Waldron puts it: ". . . anyone who knows Asian religion will instantly see that Falun Gong fits into a tradition that extends back before the beginning of recorded history." What made Falun Gong stand out from other qigong exercises and meditation practices was a moral system—compassion, truthfulness, and forbearance—unmistakably Buddhist in origin.

The revivalist aspect helps explain why Falun Gong insist on being called "practitioners," rather than "followers." Actually, they don't follow well. Ask 10 Falun Gong practitioners for a definition of Falun Gong, and you will get 10 different answers and 10 days of heated discussions. Yet it was that same do-it-yourself mentality that allowed Falun Gong to attract 70 million practitioners and skip over the barriers of Chinese society: class, education, rural/urban, civilian/military, and Party membership.

Go back to 1995, and follow a diminutive old woman around Yuyuantan Park in West Beijing. Ding Jing was a Falun Gong coordinator, meaning she taught the exercises, and kept practice sites clean. Among the sites were three locations: One catered to employees from China Central Television; two, the Xinhua News Agency; the third—very well-attended—attracted Party officials, their wives, and employees of the Public Security Bureau. From a Marxist perspective, which venerates the seizure of power using the same template, Ding's tidy practice sites represented something terrifying. In 1996, Zhuan Falun, in essence, the Falun Gong bible, was taken out of print.

Given the amorphous floating world in which they traveled—a world without membership lists, central authority or hierarchy—practitioners didn't panic. But Luo Gan, the head of the Public Security Bureau, began to use Falun Gong's perceived infiltration of his own department to gather, report, and study. Where no hierarchy existed, the Party, seizing on small clues such as Jing's phone calls to other practitioners, would map one. Where no political objectives existed, the Party would create them.

Until 1997, the Chinese media stayed neutral. Local Party leaders would show up at Falun Dafa day rallies, and chuck little children on the chin while the cameras rolled. Now critical language began to appear in the Party-controlled media—flares in the night sky indicating that the Party was trying something out.

Falun Gong had a method to handle this. Show up en masse. Stay silent. Then stand around until someone talks to you. The technique smoothly reversed various negative reports—articles in 1997, a Beijing TV segment in 1998.

In Tianjin 1999, it failed. I've made my article "An Occurrence on Fuyou Street" available. Employing interviews from both sides, it tracks the events from Tianjin on April 22 to Beijing on April 25. Essentially, the demonstration was a set-up. From the portable surveillance cameras on Fuyou Street, to the armed military unit at the Forbidden City, it was a Party bait-and-switch to create momentum for a State-level crackdown.

A former district-level official, "Minister X," recalls that the Party's decision to eliminate Falun Gong circulated internally long before any public ban, and he was told to stop granting business licenses to practitioners. A Falun Gong source saw a similar communiqué at Qinghua University in 1998. A former official of the 6–10 Office, the secret agency created to eliminate Falun Gong, noting the level of detail in practitioner files, believes that operations must have begun by 1998.

Without understanding the initial integration of Falun Gong into the Party, and the Party's initiative in starting the war—essentially creating the dilemma that threatens them today—one cannot understand the ineffectiveness of the Falun Gong response. Practitioners wanted to believe that it was a misunderstanding. So appearances at the petition office and signed letters were followed by mass detentions and the first deaths in custody.

Beginning in 2000, based on the safe house occupancy in Beijing, I estimate that well over 150,000 practitioners made their way to Tiananmen Square to protest over a year's time. Collectively, a remarkable number, but they trickled in at 500 to 1,000 per day, and they stood up and unfurled their banners according to the dictates of their soul rather than any preconceived strategy. Would a mass strategy have even been possible? I have provided another article, "Hacker Nation," on 6–10 surveillance:

> Before 1999, Falun Gong practitioners hadn't systematically used the Internet as an organizing tool. But now that they were isolated, fragmented and searching for a way to organize and change government policy, they jumped online, employing code-words, avoiding specifics, communicating in short bursts. But like a cat listening to mice squeak in a pitch black house, the "Internet Spying" Section of the 6–10 Office could find their exact location, having developed the ability to search and spy as a result of . . . a joint venture between the Shandong province public security bureau and Cisco Systems.

Following capture and initial interrogation under the 6–10 Office, the *laogai* system then operated to break the will and "transform" the practitioner, culminating with a public renunciation of Falun Gong. But it was within the *laogai* itself that the first effective resistance began.

Wang Yuzhi was a tough, successful Beijing businesswoman. When the crackdown started she transformed her office into a secret Falun Gong printing press. It was broken up, her assets were seized, Wang ran, and was eventually caught.

The low-ball casualty figure of over 3,000 practitioners who have died by torture is reasonably well-documented. Some practitioners simply refused to renounce their belief; others hoped that overcrowded prisons might contribute to the end of the persecution. Others wanted to set an example to fellow inmates.

But Wang made it personal—so personal that some of the guards force-feeding her began wearing paper bag masks so she couldn't identify them. It became a chess game between the practitioner and the torturers. Both sides knew that Wang's screams of rage were legendary throughout the *laogai* , with rumors seeping out to practitioners scattered throughout the world. Both sides knew that checkmate—actually killing Wang—would leave a pyrrhic victory for the state.

The underlying ambiguity of the *laogai* position was expressed in the following local maneuver: Rather than writing up a report of transformation failure, or the euphemism "death by suicide," many labor camps and psychiatric centers would wait until the torture reached lethal levels, and then suddenly free the dying practitioner—especially after the so-called Tiananmen "self-immolation" and the Changchun television hijacking (and I welcome questions on those incidents).

But Wang Yuzhi lived. Considered terminal on release, she fled China, and went on to purchase printing presses for the Epoch Times. Today she will smile at you with her one good eye. This is the face of insurgency, and to such a face, the Party turned to a more permanent solution.

The final article that I have made available, "China's Gruesome Organ Harvest," documents a pattern of retail-organs-only physical examinations carried out throughout the *laogai* system. I can find no rational medical explanation for the procedures, and I conclude that the commercial harvesting of Falun Gong is real. That finding has been confirmed by a Taiwanese surgeon who arranges transplants in China.

One addition: While the Bush Administration's consistent focus on House Christians may have had a Schindler's List effect, inhibiting widespread harvesting of Christians, members of one sect, Eastern Lightning, were examined for harvesting. According to interviews by my colleague Jaya Gibson, so were some Tibetan prisoners. Yet harvesting of political and religious prisoners probably began in Xinjiang. A Uyghur policeman witnessed preparation for a procedure in 1994, and I recently interviewed a Uyghur surgeon who, in 1995, was ordered to take his medical team into the outskirts of Urumqi and remove a prisoner's organs while the heart was still beating.

Perhaps harvesting began as a purely black-market operation. But ultimately prisoners who would not transform—the Wang Yuzhi types—became too dangerous to release. But the Party had an outlet, the organ tourists of Japan, Europe, and the United States.

Now the fact that China is the one currently pulling the reins up on Western organ tourism highlights Falun Gong's stunning lack of success in making its case in the United States. For many in the Bush administration, it took one outburst from Wang Wenyi on the White House Lawn to establish that Falun Gong could not be reliable allies. For many Democrats, it took one Chinese-planted Wikipedia reference alleging Falun Gong was anti-gay to ward off sympathy (Falun Gong teachings on this point are essentially indistinguishable from traditional Christianity, Judaism, Islam, and Buddhism).

Practitioners in the West simultaneously watch two screens, a Western one and a Chinese one. But for them, China is always the default—and fear of the Party's manipulative abilities runs deep. Hence we see the definitional problems, the alienating public torture displays and Daoist demarcations of good and evil—again, aimed at the mainland.

But Falun Gong's tunnel vision created one unprecedented success. Along with the construction of the greatest dissident media apparatus in modern Chinese history, a small group of Falun Gong engineers based out of a North Carolina suburb devised an Internet-lifeline to transmit information in and out of China. Along the way, they facilitated the only unblocked Internet transmissions out of Iran during the aborted Green Revolution.

If the press is correct, the State Department is considering awarding these engineers (now known as the Global Internet Freedom Consortium), significant funding to do more. If my Falun Gong sources are correct, the Consortium is concerned about taking a sum too small to make a difference, in exchange for the inevitable Party propaganda point that they are U.S. agents.

Yet the Party is pushing the two sides together. The State Department must end Chinese hacking by threatening China's Big Brother Internet. Falun Gong has perhaps a million in captivity. As much as 1 out of 10 may have already been lost to the surgical knife.

The answer to this dilemma will not be found in parsing Wikipedia. The question is no longer—What is Falun Gong? How do they define themselves? But rather—What are Falun Gong's actions? What has Falun Gong achieved? Against what sort of odds? And here, I believe the evidence of a decade—from the *laogai* to the North Carolina suburbs—speaks for itself.

———

PREPARED STATEMENT OF MARK CHUANHANG SHAN

JUNE 18, 2010

The roundtable host, the CECC, asks that "what factors influence the Chinese Government's policies toward spiritual movements and drive its treatment of members of spiritual groups. The Chinese Government has allowed space for some spiritual movements to operate in China, but has banned other groups, such as Falun Gong. Why does the Chinese Government consider some spiritual movements a threat?"

The above questions touch the root of Chinese political-religious culture. Through an analysis on the origin of the traditional political concept of the Mandate of Heaven and its modern applications, and the case of severe persecution of the Christian lawyer Gao Zhisheng because of his defending the religious freedom of Falun Gong movement, we may gain more understanding of the rational of the current Chinese political-religious culture.

I. "THE MANDATE OF HEAVEN" IN TRADITIONAL CHINESE POLITICAL IDEOLOGY

When the Zhou king's advisors persuaded him to attack the Shang dynasty (1766–1045 B.C.) he refused saying, "you do not know the Mandate of Heaven yet," but he launched the invasion after he heard Shang king did horrible things to his people as a tyrant because that showed the disapproval of Heaven of the Shang king, and Heaven began to support the Zhou king to replace the former.[1]

After the conquest, the Zhou dynasty (1045–256 B.C.) issued a number of proclamations, preserved in the Classic of Documents, persuading the Shang people to submit to their conquerors in the name of Mandate of Heaven. Zhou rulers argued that:

> Heaven, charged certain good men with rulership over the lineages of the world, and the heirs of these men might continue to exercise the Heaven-sanctioned power for as long as they carried out their religious and administrative duties with piety, rightness, and wisdom. But if the worth of the ruling family declined, if the rulers turned their backs upon the spirits and abandoned the virtuous ways that had originally marked them as worthy of the mandate to rule, then Heaven might discard them to elect a new family or lineage to be the destined rulers of the world.[2]

The later historians such as Sima Qian and thinkers such as Confucius and Mozi interpreted the Mandate of Heaven as a justification to overthrow evil rulers and start a new dynasty.[3] Therefore, the concept proved to have lasting influence and fit neatly into the later scheme of the Chinese dynastic cycles, "because it justified all successful overthrows just as it justified all dynasties that clung to power."[4] In this theoretical frame, many historical events are judged as the outcome of Divine favor or disfavor including natural signs and disasters.[5]

In Chinese history, the emperors may hold different religious faiths personally, such as Buddhism, Daoism or even Nestorian/Catholic Christianity, but the Mandate of Heaven stayed as an unchangeable law in political ideology to justify their governance.

In modern Chinese history, the great revolt against Qing Dynasty by the Christian sect "The Kingdom of Heavenly Peace Movement" (1850–1864) was led by Hong Xiuquan who viewed himself as "the second son of God" and "the younger brother of Jesus Christ" sent by God to eradicate demons and demon worship and "the overthrow of the Manchu would help bring in the Kingdom of Heaven on earth."[6] Sun Zhongshan (Sun Yat-sen 1866–1925) was a Christian and the first president of the Republic of China (1912–1949). He was a founder of the Guoming Party and in his process of overthrowing the Qiang dynasty referenced the book of Exodus in the Bible and spoke of Jesus as a liberator who motivated him as he said "Moses did that, I can too," and "Jesus is a revolutionary, so am I," etc.[7] He also claimed that "God sent him to struggle with evil for the Chinese . . . and liberating Chinese from bondage."[8] He also said "I am a Christian having fought demons more than forty years . . ."[9] The concept the Mandate of Heaven has even survived into the Communist China. For example, during the 1989 student movement which led to the Tian-an-men Square massacre, "many commentators remarked that the Communist Party has lost the Mandate of Heaven."[10]

Because of this spiritual feature of the political concept, spiritual or religious movements in Chinese history make it easy to challenge ruling of dynasties through spiritual moral approaches, thus Chinese Governments are sensitive to the political-spiritual touch and are not tolerant of any spiritual movements shaking their ruling authority before the Chinese people. In addition, Chinese Governments have tended to keep state and religion separated through promoting non-religious Confucianism throughout much of their history, and that is an efficient way to keep religious or spiritual movements out of politics.

II. AN ANALYSIS OF DIFFERENT DEGREES OF FREEDOM AND SUPPRESSION OF CURRENT SPIRITUAL-RELIGIOUS MOVEMENTS IN CHINA, AND THE PERSECUTION CASE OF CHRISTIAN LAWYER GAO ZHISHENG[11] (REFER TO CECC SUBMISSION 1, 2: STORY OF GAO ZHISHENG)

"The legal existence of the religious complexities totally relies on the co-operation and the acceptance of the leadership with the government, and the government grasps the very final right to choose the partnership." (Ding, August 1995. Volume 15, No. 88)[12]

Though the Chinese Communist government is strongly atheist without believing in any spiritual things they are still sensitive to any spiritual movements that touch on politics being seen as a way of challenging their authority. On the other hand, the government tries hard to leave more room for those spiritual religions that respect their authority and abide by the religious policies, mostly in a way of promoting patriotic nationalism today. For instance, the Protestant Christian House Churches and Catholic Christian Underground Churches are persecuted, but the Protestant and Catholic Churches in the official Three-self Patriotic System (or TSPM) enjoy more freedom. Tibetan Buddhism is under suppression because of its feature of religion-politics combination, but Buddhism and Daoism in other parts of China enjoy comparatively much more freedom because they touch no politics. Islam among Uyghurs is under suppression because of the Xinjiang political problem, but Islam among Hui enjoys more freedom. This is true, not only inside same spiritual traditions, but also if we compare government treatments among different spiritual movements or religions in China.

Similarly, the Qi-gong Movement has many branches. Some were suppressed but others are allowed more freedom. A Qi-gong branch, the Zhong-gong, was also suppressed and its leader Zhang Hongbao before his death in 2006 established a shadow government of China in the United States. Falun Gong, another branch of Qi-gong Movement, in its siege of the Party headquarters in Beijing on April 25, 1999, by more than 20,000 Falun Gong practitioners, was the main factor for the Chinese Government to crackdown against the Falun Gong.[13] The large number of public protest challenges to the government touched on politics seriously. One of Falun Gong's protest slogans after they went abroad is "Heaven Eliminates Chinese Community Party" which is an interpretation of the concept of the Mandate of Heaven.

Among human rights Christian lawyers in China Gao Zhisheng received the most serious inhuman persecution because he was an attorney defending the religious freedom and human rights of some Falun Gong practitioners. The Falun Gong movement was suppressed more than other spiritual movements in China as CECC has pointed out. Therefore, when Gao Zhisheng did not gave up representing the Falun Gong members in China, the government attack of revenge on him has become severe.

At this roundtable, CECC also asks: "what does the Chinese Government's treatment of spiritual movements mean for the future of religious freedom in China?"

The sociologist Yang Fenggang proposes a Triple-color Market Model to analyze the religious situation in contemporary China: "a red market (officially permitted religions), a black market (officially banned religions), and a gray market (religions with an ambiguous legal/illegal status). The gray market concept accentuates non-institutionalized religiosity (2006, Purdue University)." His three propositions are: "to the extent that religious organizations are restricted in number and in operation, a black market will emerge in spite of high costs to individuals; to the extent that a red market is restricted and a black market is suppressed, a gray market will emerge; the more restrictive and suppressive the regulation, the larger the gray market."[14]

This model can be applied to conditions in China today by stating that a red market means that religions or spiritual movements which do not touch on politics have the most freedom (e.g. non-Tibetan Buddhism and Daoism); a black market means that banned ones (such as Falun Gong) which do touch on politics in a way of challenging the Communist government authority suffer the most suppression. A gray market ambiguous in their political interest, such as non-institutionalized Protestant House Church Christianity (Catholic Underground Church is closer to the black market because of its political feature extended from the Vatican), will continue to grow larger as others are encouraged or suppressed.

III. CONCLUSION WITH A SPECULATIVE ANALYSIS ON THE ROLE OF CHRISTIANITY FOR FUTURE OF RELIGIOUS FREEDOM IN CHINA

Chinese Governments through the history have not tolerated spiritual or religious movements which "touch on politics" because the moral claims they hold make it easy to powerfully challenge the authority of the government through the concept of the Mandate of Heaven when a government does not benefit all the people or is seen as corrupt.

Interesting to note, Christians in China see in the Bible the mandate to pray for the government to prosper so that they may prosper also.[15] While the Protestant Christian House Churches maintain spiritual and moral standards of behavior and its church setting teachings emphasize "we do not touch politics,"[16] "blessed are those who are persecuted for righteousness" or even "love your enemies and pray for those who persecute you (Matthew 5:10,44)" as the followers of Jesus Christ, they are not a direct political threat to government and seem to have a bright future in China even under attempts of the government to restrict or suppress them. One important reason for the tighter restriction and suppression is the lesson learned by Chinese Government from Eastern Europe's Communist regimes which collapsed with Christianity playing an indirect role.

The founder and president of ChinaAid Association with the mission of help the persecuted churches and promote religious freedom in China, Bob Fu, a pastor and theologian, pointed out that "House churches which are committed to the sole headship of Christ in the church and to evangelism must operate as illegal groups conducting so-called 'illegal religious activities,' and consequently must suffer the administrative penalties inflicted by the state." [17]

Together Christianity in the gray market House Church and the red market TSPM Church is transforming the condition of religious freedom in China through the "new non-institutionalized religious citizen community" [18] established in the whole nation.

(Refer to CECC Submission 3: 2009 Annual Report of ChinaAid Association.)

---

[1] Valerie Hansen, The Open Empire, a history of China to 1600, (New York-London: W. W. Norton & Company, 2000), 40–41.

[2] Compiled by WM. Theodore de Bary and Irene Bloom, Source of Chinese Tradition, Volume I, from earliest times to 1600, (New York: Columbia University Press, 1999), 27.

[3] Valerie Hansen., 41.

[4] Ibid.

[5] Ibid.

[6] Richard Hooker, Ch'ing China: The Taiping Rebellion, http://www.wsu.edu/dee/CHING/TAIPING.HTM

[7] Wang Zhongxin, Sun Zhongshan and Christianity, Christianity and China, Volume IV, (The Blessings Foundation, Inc. CA, USA), 15.

[8] Ibid.

[9] Ibid., 15–16.

[10] Valerie Hansen., 41.

[11] More information on www.freealim.com

[12] cf. Bob Fu, God and Caesar: Church and State Relations in Communist China, Professor in Religion and Philosophy at Oklahoma Wesleyan University for the 2003–2005 academic years.

[13] James W. Tong, Revenge of the Forbidden City: The Suppression of the Falungong in China, 1999–2005.

[14] Fenggang Yang, The Red, Black, and Gray Markets of Religion In China, The Sociological Quarterly 47 (2006) 93–122 © 2006 Μιδςεστ Σοψιολογιψαλ Σοψιετυ.

[15] Jeremiah 29:7 "Also seek the peace and prosperity of the city to which I have carried you into exile. Pray to the Lord for it, because if it proper, you too will prosper." See also, Romans 13:5–6 "Therefore, it is necessary to submit to the authorities, not only because of possible punishment but also because of conscience . . . for the authorities are God's servants . . ."

[16] When Bob Fu was arrested and interrogated in Beijing 1996 because his leadership of a house church, he answered the police after he was put in the jail: "I didn't preach anything about politics in our church, because I believe the separation of the church and state." The police answered: "I want you to know that you must talk politics everywhere." That meant the government wants the house church to support the communist politics everywhere.

[17] Bob Fu, God and Caesar: Church and State Relations in Communist China.

[18] ChinaAid Association, 2009 Annual Report of Persecution by the Government on Christian House Churches within Mainland China, Part V 1. Church as a Corner Stone of Chinese Citizen Society.

SUBMISSION FOR THE RECORD #1

Excerpt from www.FreeGao.com

"Christian human rights Attorney Gao Zhisheng was seized by a dozen police officers and last seen in public on February 4, 2009. Gao has been repeatedly kidnapped, arrested, imprisoned and tortured by Chinese authorities for defending the persecuted. He has been an unyielding and iconic advocate for justice in the Chinese courts and was even nominated for the Nobel Peace Prize in 2008.

On January 21, 2010, the Chinese Government publicly acknowledged Gao Zhisheng to be in their custody, for the first time since his abduction more than 365 days ago. In response to a reporter's inquiry, Chinese Foreign Ministry Spokesperson Ma Zhaoxu said: "The relevant judicial authorities have decided this case, and we should say this person, according to Chinese law, is where he should be." Mr. Ma then added, "As far as what exactly he's doing, I don't know. You can ask the relevant authorities."

The Ministry's comments brought a glimmer of hope to Gao supporters around the world. Since December 2009, rumors of Gao's death from torture in prison have spread uncertainty. Just one week before Mr. Ma spoke to the media, Gao's older brother, Gao Zhiyi, was informed by a police officer that Gao Zhisheng had gotten "lost and went missing while out on a walk" in September, 2009. The news of his death, then alleged disappearance, devastated Gao's wife and children.

Finally, on January 20, 2010, an Australian newspaper reported from an inside source that "Gao is still alive at present . . . he's not missing."

SUBMISSION FOR THE RECORD #2

Excerpt from ChinaAid's newsletter, distributed by ChinaAid on May 10, 2010, via email

"ChinaAid thanks you for your continued support of Gao Zhisheng. We have learned that Gao was last seen on April 15–16 visiting his in-laws in Xinjiang. He did not return to his Beijing apartment the following week, as he was scheduled to according to the family. He has not been seen or heard from him since.

"ChinaAid is actively searching for Gao and news of his condition and whereabouts. With no news in over three weeks, we fear Gao Zhisheng has been forced to disappear again. We will continue to press for information, and keep all Gao supporters updated with the latest confirmed news. We thank you for your continued prayers and support for Gao Zhisheng, and will not relent until Gao has been released, and is able to reunite with his family in the United States.

"As we continue to press for Gao Zhisheng, ChinaAid remains committed to defending other persecuted faithfuls in China. Hundreds of thousands suffer persecution for their faith, and in extreme cases, like that of Uyghur Christian Alimujiang Yimiti, it takes a global effort to call for justice."

SUBMISSION FOR THE RECORD #3

Excerpt from the 2009 ChinaAid "Annual Report of Persecution by the Government on Christian House Churches within Mainland China," Part V, Section 1. Church as a Corner Stone of Chinese Citizen Society

"In his classical book "Citizenship and Social Class" (1964), T. H. Marshall defined modern citizenship as "a personal status consisting of a body of universal rights, i.e., legal claims on the state, and the duties held equally by all legal members of a nation-state (Marshall; Brubaker 1992)." He also defined three basic rights of modern citizenship: civil rights, political rights and social rights.

Many scholars agree that the legal requirements for an emergent capitalist society were chiefly responsible for the birth of modern citizenship rights and that "the struggle to extend citizenship in the nineteenth and twentieth centuries was carried on primarily by English working class through such important democratic movements as Chartism, the Factory Movement, and trade unionism," yet Margaret R. Somers argues that the "social and political movements of those tumultuous industrializing epochs were built primarily on the efforts, political identities, and social activities of rural industrial working peoples in the pastoral regions (Somers 1993, Michigan University)." For Somers, "varying patterns of institutional relationships among law, communities and political culture were central factors in shaping modern citizenship rights," and she argues that citizenship as an instituted process rather than a status."

To apply the above theories to China, we should admit that Chinese society is just starting to evolve into a citizenship society. Based on the 2009 report of persecution on House Church Movement in China, we also need to add religious rights, which were not such a concern for 19th and 20th century Christian Europe, to the three citizenship rights listed above. Then, to apply these four central rights theory we can see three major elements in the institutional process contributing to the construction of a Chinese citizenship society based on the emerging national capitalism since 1979. In the last 20 years these have been: the Western Law infrastructure borrowed by China, a Church Movement Community, as well as traditional symbolic political culture originating in Communist ideology, Confucianism and other ideas, which have stimulated needs for citizenship (Shan Chuanhang, 2008, Boston University, with an acknowledgment to Dr. Nancy Ammerman). The community used to be in the three major elements formula was an intellectual one but it faded away from the instituted process after 1989's brutal suppression and replaced by church movement community.

The Christian communities (mostly House Church Movement and Three-Self Church) in China grew fast in an invisible model because of persecution, yet it emerges as a new social and spiritual block in society, through not giving up meeting together. Beijing Shouwang, Shanghai Wanbang, Chengdu Qiuyu zhifu and Guangdong Liangren house churches were all typical examples in 2009 of churches that did not give up meeting together under severe pressure from the government. Christian communities, similarly to the pastoral regions of Europe in 19th and 20th centuries, can also shape powerfully a Chinese citizenship society with a possible future "plausibility structure" (Peter L. Berger, 1966, Boston University).

————

PREPARED STATEMENT OF SARAH COOK

JUNE 18, 2010

Good afternoon.

One of the topics I've been asked to speak about is the story of Gao Zhisheng, a leading Chinese human rights lawyer and vocal advocate for religious freedom, particularly for Falun Gong practitioners. Several years ago I had the honor of co-editing the English translation of Gao Zhisheng's memoir A China More Just. So, as I was considering how to begin today, I tried to think of what Gao would say if he were here today himself. There are two points that he would probably emphasize.

First, he would give a heartfelt thank you. Thank you to the Commission for organizing this panel. Thank you to the United States government for taking an active interest in the human rights abuses taking place in China. Thank you to those in the audience who care for the Chinese people.

Second, he would likely seek to convey the urgency of the current situation and the brutality of the treatment suffered by large numbers of Chinese people generally, but also of Falun Gong practitioners in particular. It is clear from his writings that the account after account of severe torture he heard from the Falun Gong victims he had interviewed left a profound impression on him and served as a key catalyst in his advocacy on their behalf.

> With a trembling heart and a trembling pen, I record the tragic experiences of those [Falun Gong practitioners] who have been persecuted in the last six years. Of all the true accounts of incredible violence that I have heard, of all the records of the government's inhuman torture of its own people, what has shaken me most is the routine practice of assaulting women's genitals. Almost all who have been persecuted, be they male or female, were stripped naked before being tortured. No words can describe our government's vulgarity and immorality.[1]

While not spoken in quite such colorful language, Freedom House's findings generally reflect what Gao had discovered.

But before moving onto some specific details, I'd like to take a step back to address the question of why this is happening and to point out that the repression of Falun Gong and spiritual movements in China cannot be viewed in a vacuum. Rather, it is part of an elaborate machinery of suppression that arbitrarily and systemically denies independent thought and expression in a range of areas in Chinese society. Moreover, Freedom House's findings indicate that this repression is, in some respects, getting worse.

In the past few decades, the Communist Party's tactics for suppressing free thought have become more sophisticated. But the underlying principle and institutional dynamic remains the same: the decision of what is approved or forbidden is made arbitrarily by Party leaders and that decision is generally based on their perception of threats to their monopoly on political power or legitimacy, whether these threats are real or imagined. This dynamic is reflected in every set of media censorship directives issued by the Communist Party's Propaganda Department that gets leaked and posted online, but it applies equally to spiritual movements.

Thus, whatever the specific timeline of events in the mid to late 1990s, one angle for explaining the banning of Falun Gong and other smaller spiritual groups is that Party leaders did so: a. because they could and there was no institutional mechanism like an independent judiciary to stop them; and b. because the Communist Party generally has a low tolerance for groups or individuals who place any authority, spiritual or otherwise, above their allegiance to the Party.

For persecuted Tibetans, this authority is the Dalai Lama; for persecuted human rights lawyers—whom I'll get to in a moment—it is the law; for persecuted Falun

Gong adherents, it is the dedication to spiritual teachings centered on the values of truthfulness, compassion, and tolerance. The Party's emphasis on "transforming" Falun Gong practitioners—similar to its "patriotic education" campaigns in Tibet—is one indication of this pursuit of suppressing independent thought.

Since 1999, Freedom House's annual and other publications have recorded the ongoing rights abuses suffered by those who practice Falun Gong in China. Several aspects of the persecution stand out from a review of those findings. I'll mention them briefly here and am happy to followup on in more detail during the Q and A.

- *First, large scale detentions and widespread surveillance.* These appeared to intensify in 2008 and 2009 even from the already high levels experienced over the past decade. Falun Gong practitioners were a key target in what amounted to a broader crackdown surrounding the Olympics and a series of politically sensitive anniversaries. In addition to detention and monitoring, this phenomenon included regular citation in official statements on "strike hard" campaigns and in offers of monetary rewards to members of the public for turning in individuals distributing information related to Falun Gong.
- *Second, ongoing torture and deaths in custody.* While Freedom House does not have the resources to maintain a comprehensive record of such deaths, well-documented individual cases come to light each year, while overseas Falun Gong groups have gathered detailed accounts of over 3,000 people killed in the last decade. In one high-profile case from 2008, Beijing musician Yu Zhou died in custody 11 days after being detained for possessing Falun Gong literature in late January; his wife, Xu Na, was sentenced in November to three years in prison.[2] In January 2009, Chongqing resident Jiang Xiqing died while held at a "reeducation through labor" camp for practicing Falun Gong; lawyers seeking to investigate his death were detained and beaten.[3]
- *Third, the sentencing of practitioners to long prison terms following unfair trials or to "reeducation through labor" camps by bureaucratic fiat.* Based on interviews with recently released detainees, a February 2009 study by the Chinese Human Rights Defenders group reported that in addition to petty thieves and drug addicts, Falun Gong practitioners constituted a significant percentage of those incarcerated in the camps, as did Christians in some facilities.[4] Given a nationwide labor camp population numbering in the hundreds of thousands, if not more, and former prisoners' accounts of hundreds of religious prisoners in individual camps, this translates into potentially tens of thousands of detainees.
- *Fourth, Falun Gong is a permanent taboo for Chinese media outlets and one of the most systematically censored topics on the Internet.* In addition to the well-known use of technical filtering to block access to Falun Gong-related websites, tests conducted as part of a recent Freedom House study of Internet freedom in China found that entries containing the keyword "Falun Gong" (as well as "June 4" or the "Dalai Lama") could not be displayed on Chinese blog hosting services, including the simplified Chinese version of Microsoft's MSN Space Live service and Skype's Chinese version, Tom.[5]

Those who seek to spread information despite these restrictions risk detention and imprisonment. Several well-documented cases have emerged in recent years of Chinese citizens imprisoned simply for downloading, printing, or possessing Falun Gong-related materials, either for their personal use or for sharing with others. These included victims who were not Falun Gong practitioners. For example:

- In November 2008, Liu Jin, a former university librarian, was sentenced to three years in prison in Shanghai after she downloaded information about Falun Gong from the Internet and passed it to others, which her lawyer argued was a common occurrence.[6]
- In March 2009, Zhang Xingwu, a retired professor and Falun Gong practitioner from Shandong province, was sentenced to seven years in prison after security forces broke into his home and confiscated VCDs and religious texts related to Falun Gong.[7]
- Last month, grassroots democracy activist Ren Ming from Shenzhen was reportedly sentenced to three years in prison for distributing CDs bearing a Falun Gong symbol.[8]

It is in this context of a persecuted religious minority facing large scale, brutal treatment from the authorities on the one hand, and silence, if not cooperation, from most of society on the other, that Gao Zhisheng and other lawyers' efforts to represent Falun Gong practitioners become relevant.

As brief background on Gao, he was born in rural Shaanxi province and grew up in his mother's cave dwelling. In the late 1980s, he was selling vegetables on the streets of Xinjiang province when he came across and advertisement that the government was seeking to train lawyers. So, with just a middle school education, he decided to teach himself and in 1995, he passed the bar exam. In addition to his regular cases, he immediately started taking pro bono ones for the gamut of China's vulnerable groups. He soon became known nationwide and in 2001, was named one of China's top 10 lawyers after a legal debate competition sponsored by the Ministry of Justice.

It was in this context that in 2004, Gao was one of the first lawyers to break the Falun Gong taboo. He was hired by an adherent who had been sent to a labor camp and was stunned that judges repeatedly rejected his efforts to file for judicial review. He writes about visiting multiple courts in one day and being told by three judges: "Don't you know we don't take Falun Gong cases?" With legal avenues closed, Gao decided to write an open letter to the National People's Congress and a few months later, he conducted the first of two in depth investigations into the persecution of Falun Gong. In October and December 2005, he wrote two open letters to Hu Jintao and Wen Jiabao, detailing the torture he had uncovered and urging them to end the atrocities.

In response, as many here probably know, he and his family were put under escalating pressure and abuse themselves: from 24-hour surveillance to having his law firm shut down and license revoked, to an attempt on his life and repeated incommunicado detentions. In December 2006, Gao was sentenced in a one day trial to three years in prison. But this was suspended and the Chinese authorities have instead used "disappearance" rather than imprisonment as their preferred tactic against him.

It was only in February 2009, that, in an incredible feat of courage, we learned the full details of the torture he had suffered during his previous detention. In a letter he managed to send abroad, Gao chronicled being stripped naked and shocked with electric batons on his genitals, among other acts torture. Guards reportedly told him that the conclusions of his investigations were accurate and that these were indeed the torture methods "perfected" on Falun Gong practitioners, all the while pressuring him that if he simply said a few negative comments about Falun Gong and/or praise to the Party, the torture would cease.[9] Almost immediately with the release of the letter, Gao was abducted again. His family managed to flee China to Thailand, but Gao remained "disappeared" throughout much of 2009. As the months went on, his family, friends, and fellow lawyers grew increasingly fearful that he had been killed in custody. In March 2010, the authorities allowed him to resurface following an intense international campaign on his behalf. But after the international limelight faded, he disappeared again in April. He hasn't been heard from since.

Ironically perhaps, Gao never actually had the opportunity to argue in defense of a Falun Gong client in court. But, at least 20 lawyers have followed in his footsteps and done so. In response, they too have been temporarily or permanently disbarred, beaten, abducted, shocked with electric batons, held in a cage at a police station, and in at least one case, imprisoned for seven years under the same arbitrary and vague legal provision used to justify imprisonment of his Falun Gong clients.

The authorities' mistreatment of these lawyers reflects two broader implications of the campaign against certain spiritual groups for the future development of religious freedom and rule of law in China.

First, the tactics and strategies developed to suppress one group can be quickly and easily applied to others. From vague legal provisions, to "black jails," to certain torture and "transformation" methods, the lawyers and others have remarked on how elements first used against Falun Gong practitioners are then applied to other victim groups, including the lawyers themselves. It is evident from the writings and comments of Gao and other lawyers that the reason they take such a risk defending Falun Gong and other persecuted religious believers is because they feel very strongly that if the current system is not able to protect these innocent people from such severe abuses, others are at risk as well.

Second, the Communist Party's intransigent and harsh response to these lawyers highlights its general reluctance to institute genuine rule of law. Indeed, as Jerome Cohen has repeatedly noted in his writings, in the past two years there appears to have been a backsliding on even previous, limited reforms, while Party control over the judicial system has tightened.

This reality raises complex questions of what actions the United States government and other members of the international community might be able to take to improve the situation for individuals like Gao or Falun Gong practitioners. While not comprehensive, I hope that the following three recommendations may prove helpful as a starting point for such a discussion:

1. Continue to lobby for the release of individual prisoners of conscience: As harshly as Gao Zhisheng has been treated by Chinese security forces, there is little doubt that his situation would be even more dire without the intense international pressure that has been applied to the Chinese regime on his behalf. Other former prisoners whom I have interviewed and who were the subject of international appeal campaigns—including Falun Gong practitioners—have repeatedly testified to the noticeably less harsh treatment they received compared to their fellow, more internationally anonymous, detainees.

2. Support initiatives to independently research and verify more individual cases: Central to the ability to advocate on behalf of individuals and to gauge the full scale of abuses targeting spiritual movements is the capacity to verify individual cases of religious prisoners. Despite the sensitivity of the issue and difficulty in obtaining information about Falun Gong or Christian prisoners, there are avenues for doing so. Increased support, including funding, for groups taking the initiative to compile credible prisoner lists could translate into real protection for members of these persecuted minorities.

3. Remain vigilant in the face of Chinese official pressure to self-censor outside of China: Although this is not the focus of today's discussion, pressure to self-censor beyond China's borders is a daily reality for Falun Gong practitioners—similar to Tibetans, Uighurs, and others—who seek to organize events that might expose abuses in China or challenge the Communist Party's dominant narrative about the country's current reality. It is critical that outside China, hosts of cultural, academic, or other events be vigilant in protecting the right to free expression for all, including those whose voices are systematically silenced within China.

There is one last point I'd like to make before I conclude—on a more optimistic note. Parallel to the increased repression we've seen in China in the past few years has been a growing rights consciousness on the part of ordinary citizens. Indeed, one might argue, the insecurity of the regime in the face of a more assertive citizenry is one reason for the expanded repressive apparatus. As with workers, bloggers, and journalists, Falun Gong practitioners have also been among those using incredible ingenuity, creativity, and courage to challenge the repression against them, primarily by trying to convince fellow citizens of the justice of their cause.

Having begun with quoting Gao, I'd like to conclude with a few his words on the potential affect of their efforts.

> More and more people around me, including professionals, scholars, government staff members, and ordinary Chinese citizens have begun to question the rationale behind the campaign against these believers. This has been a palpable change. . . . These people have come to realize how unjust, inhumane, and lawless the government's violent persecution of the Falun Gong people is. This rapid, widespread change in attitude stands in stark contrast to the government's static, outdated practice. It is really quite thought-provoking." [10]

I hope that at some point in the future, Gao will be able to be here himself to speak these words. Thank you.

---

[1] Gao Zhisheng, A China More Just, Broad Press USA (2007); pg. 137

[2] Freedom House, "China," Freedom in the World 2009: http://www.freedomhouse.org/template.cfm?page=363&year=2009&country=7586

[3] Freedom House, "China," Freedom in the World 2010: http://www.freedomhouse.org/template.cfm?page=22&year=2010&country=7801

[4] Chinese Human Rights Defenders, "Re-education through Labor Abuses Continue Unabated: Overhaul Long Overdue," February 2009: http://docs.law.gwu.edu/facweb/dclarke/public/CHRD—RTL—Report.pdf

[5] Freedom House, "China" Freedom on the Net 2009: http://www.freedomhouse.org/template.cfm?page=384&key=197&parent=19&report=79

[6] Ibid.

[7] Freedom House, "China," Freedom of the Press 2010 (forthcoming)

[8] Chinese Human Rights Defenders, "China Human Rights Briefing Weekly: May 18–24, 2010," May 26, 2010; available at http://blogs.amnesty.org.uk/blogs—entry.asp?eid=6592

[9] Gao Zhisheng, "A Letter from the Twenty-first Century Dungeon—Over Fifty Days of Endless Inhumane Tortures in the Hands of the Chinese Government," published by China Aid on February 9, 2009; http://chinaaid.org/pdf/Human%20Rights%20Lawyer%20Recounts%20Torture.pdf

[10] Gao Zhisheng, A China More Just, Broad Press USA (2007); pg. 86

SUBMISSION FOR THE RECORD

PREPARED STATEMENT OF CAYLAN FORD, FALUN GONG PRACTITIONER AND
VOLUNTEER ANALYST AND EDITOR, FALUN DAFA INFORMATION CENTER

JUNE 18, 2010

I would first like to thank you for the opportunity to submit this statement, and more importantly, for your efforts to shed light on this topic. My name is Caylan Ford, I am a practitioner of Falun Gong, and also a volunteer analyst and editor with the Falun Dafa Information Center. Today I would like to speak to the question of how Falun Gong perceives the persecution in China today, both in terms of its origins and its meanings, as well as the forces that will contribute to its eventual end. I should add the caveat that all Falun Gong practitioners have their own interpretations and understandings of these questions, but I will do my best to illuminate broad collective understandings.

I'll first address the causes of the suppression in China. This is an issue that defies easy comprehension. Journalists, scholars, and other observers have offered a number of compelling explanations to help account for why the Chinese Communist Party viewed the peaceful and apolitical Falun Gong as such a threat. The size of the practice is the first thing that comes to mind. By 1999, widely cited government estimated put the number of Falun Gong practitioners in China in excess of 70 million people. That's larger than the membership of the Communist Party at the time, and it's likely the largest independent civil society group in the history of the PRC.

Second, Falun Gong existed outside of official sanction; in March of 1996, because Falun Gong refused to charge money for the practice and wished to exercise autonomy over its activities, it withdrew from the state-run Qigong Research Association. Subsequent attempts to register with the government in another form were rebuffed, and so Falun Gong was, for three years, a vast popular religion with no oversight by the state. Third, some of the personalities involved—namely Luo Gan and then-Party chief Jiang Zemin—were uniquely suspicious or jealous of Falun Gong's popularity, and as Willy Lam suggested in 2001, Jiang may have intended the suppression to be a means of consolidating personal power.

There are other explanations as well that place the crackdown against Falun Gong in the context of broader cycles of "fang and shou" (relaxation and tightening) in Chinese politics. That is, after a remarkable period of tolerance toward qigong practices in the 1990s, the Communist Party again sought to reign in the influence and autonomy of these groups.

All of these explanations likely contain some truth. Yet even taken together, they cannot account for the ferocity with which the suppression of Falun Gong has been pursued. For that, one must look to the very foundations of the Communist Party's rule, and understand how Falun Gong's spiritual message, however benign, undermined the sources of the Communist Party's legitimacy.

The PRC, in a sense, a kind of theocracy, only its religion is a secular one. The Party's mandate to rule derives from its claim to possess exclusive knowledge of certain Truths. The Marxist/Leninist ideology, including its vision of history and definitions of progress, serve as the ideological basis for Communist Party rule. That no one really believes in Marxism in contemporary China does not make this less so; it only means that the Party's ideological standing is more tenuous than in past decades, and its eagerness to suppress others may be more acute.

Falun Gong, and other independent religious groups, challenges the Party's ability to command faith and allegiance. The Communist Party believes in the primacy of human agency. Falun Gong believes that human agency is subordinate to divine authority. Where Mao Zedong spoke of struggling against the heavens, Falun Gong reconnects with a traditional Chinese aspiration to live in harmony with the Dao. Where Communism explains human behavior as a function of material determinism, Falun Gong's beliefs hold that human beings are innately good, that they are driven by conscience and compassion. And where the Party has sought to enhance its legitimacy over the last two decades by fostering economic growth, Falun Gong stresses that virtue is the source of true value.

For approximately one week immediately following the ban on Falun Gong, carefully crafted editorials in Xinhua and the People's Daily which explained the ban focused on Falun Gong's moral philosophy. An editorial appearing in Xinhua on July 27, 1999, proclaimed that "'truth, kindness and tolerance' principle preached by Li Hongzhi has nothing in common with the socialist ethical and cultural progress we are striving to achieve."

Another wrote that "Marxist dialectic materialism and historical materialism represent the world outlook and methodology of the proletariat, and . . . the scientific theories of Marxism established on the basis of this world view should serve as the spiritual pillar of communists. Falun Dafa as created by Li Hongzhi preaches idealism and theism . . . and thus is absolutely contradictory to the fundamental theories and principles of Marxism." And so on.

These editorials lasted little more than a week before eventually giving way to more incendiary attacks. But while they lasted, they provided a candid glimpse at why the Party viewed why Falun Gong with such trepidation. It is not because Falun Gong practitioners sought political power (they didn't), nor was it merely because of their size or independence from the state. Rather, Falun Gong offered a compelling moral philosophy, rooted in China's spiritual traditions, that was seen by Jiang Zemin as undermining the already faltering appeal of the party's ideology, and that cast the Party's moral deficiencies in stark relief.

And so, because China's rulers believed themselves to be at odds with the principles of truth, compassion, and tolerance and with the theistic spiritual orientation of Falun Gong, they have pursued its adherents with incredible resolve.

Understanding this dynamic can help answer another important question: why have so many Chinese Falun Gong adherents—tens of millions, by some estimates—persisted in exercising their faith when confronted with the full force of China's persecutory apparatus bearing down on them? Why don't they simply denounce Falun Gong? The objective of the imprisonment and the violence, after all, is forced religious conversion; if adherents recant, they are freed from detention. If they don't, they are held extrajudicially and subjected to painful punishment. And yet the choice for millions of Falun Gong adherents has been to persist in spite of the threats; to continue practicing Falun Gong, and in many cases to risk their lives in order to tell their compatriots about the persecution and the practice.

To be clear, Falun Gong practitioners don't invite martyrdom. They seek not to be tortured; they want out of labor camps. But given the choice between recanting their faith or being tortured, most still choose the latter. What motivates them?

The answer has already been alluded to. Falun Gong is suppressed because the Party fears that if people believe in divine authority, if they seek moral and personal inspiration from a religious belief system, then the Party loses control. The Communist Party dictates that a person's life belongs to the cause of Communism; a person possessed of a spiritual faith, by contrast, believes that life originates with and is connected to something which transcends this physical existence. They are thus far more impervious to control or coercion with threats, violence, with material incentives; they are their own people, their hearts and minds not the property or subject of the state.

Falun Gong's capacity to resist elimination in China lies precisely in its belief, one shared by all religions, that life goes on in the hereafter, and that the state in which you exist in the next life is connected to how you choose to live in this one. Falun Gong's faith holds that the virtues of Truth, Compassion, and Tolerance describe the intrinsic nature of the universe itself; that they are eternal and undying. And if a person seeks to live in line with these principles, they are connecting to something far greater than themselves. If a person lives a life of honesty, of courage, of compassion and justice, then in that act alone they forge something that is everlasting; they achieve a kind of immortality.

To observers who do not believe in an afterlife, who are pure pragmatists, Falun Gong's response to persecution as folly. But even if you don't believe in a life hereafter, there is still something to be said for living a life devoted to principles, or to believing that maybe virtue is its own reward. Posterity seldom remembers pragmatists. The great figures of history are men possessed of principles who made immense personal sacrifices in defense of justice. Were they pragmatists, people who put their own immediate interests ahead of principles, we would not know their names, nor would we be able to enjoy their legacy.

This explains why Falun Gong adherents have resisted suppression in China, and why they have not folded in labor camps and under threat of violence. The same rationale also explains how Falun Gong has responded to the persecution.

At some point in the last decade, you have likely encountered some manifestation of Falun Gong's response to persecution: the silent vigils of meditation kept outside Chinese embassies or consulates, the appeals of a young woman whose sister is held in a labor camp in China, or the rallies and marches meant to raise awareness of persecution in China. You have likely heard about the media outlets that some Falun Gong adherents started to provide an alternative to Chinese state-run television and newspaper, or about how software developed by American Falun Gong practitioners is now used to circumvent government censorship of the Internet from China to Iran, Syria to Burma.

Some of these activities—and especially Falun Gong practitioners' efforts to encourage people to denounce their affiliations to the Communist Party—bear distinctly political overtones. This has given rise to the belief in some circles that the Falun Gong community has become a political force in China, or even that it seeks power for itself.

But look more closely at Falun Gong's resistance and you find that it lacks the qualities of a true political movement. While most Falun Gong adherents believe that good government should be one that respects freedom of speech, of press, rule of law and that institutionalizes a separation of church and state, few of us would be likely to describe the solution to our suppression in China as lying in institutional or political change. Falun Gong has never sought to prescribe what China's government (or any other government) should look like. Its adherents do not covet political power or influence, and they do not participate in debates on other social or political issues. To put it plainly, Falun Gong adherents ascribe relatively little importance to political institutions in general.

When the persecution began, Falun Gong initially responded somewhat incredulously, believing that the authorities had simply made a mistake. These were people who based their self-identity on being law-abiding, peaceful people, and they believed that if they simply explained themselves, the suppression on Falun Gong would be lifted.

Adherents' response was characteristic of what political scientist Kevin O'Brien describes as China's "rightful resisters": people who did not want to challenge the government, but instead wanted it to uphold its own laws and protect existing social contracts. These are people who, rather than going underground to engage in subversion, sought the government's attention and made appeals to its institutions and leaders in good faith. To that end, Falun Gong practitioners from across the country traveled to local petitioning offices where they hoped to explain why Falun Gong was no threat to the government and request that their rights be restored. It did not turn out well. The local appeal offices became gateways to labor camps and prisons.

Practitioners soon began looking beyond their local government offices and toward Beijing, calling for dialogue, reconciliation, and understanding. Yet the results were no better. On any given day from late 1999 to early 2001, hundreds of Falun Gong adherents from around the country would turn up on Tiananmen Square to stage silent protests, to meditate, or to unfurl banners proclaiming Falun Dafa's goodness and innocence. They referred to these demonstrations never as protests, but as "appeals," implying that they still held out hope that the leadership would change its mind. Nonetheless, they were met with brutal reprisals, and the violence and the scale of the suppression only escalated.

In late 2001, and continuing to this day, Falun Gong adherents shifted focus. The Communist Party was committed to its course, but perhaps the people of China could be persuaded. If the people refused to be complicit, there would be no police willing to arrest practitioners, no teachers willing to turn in their students (or vice versa), no judges willing to be compromised. Denied any voice in the official media, the daily protests on Tiananmen Square gave way to autonomous underground printing houses in nearly every county and district in the country—China's equivalent of the Soviet Samizdat, one could say. From their living rooms, adherents would establish secure Internet connections, access websites outside China using proxy servers, download usually censored literature on the persecution of Falun Gong, and use it to produce homemade leaflets which they would distribute by nightfall. Falun Gong adherents living outside China worked to give scale to these efforts, creating censorship-circumvention software, launching Chinese-language radio and satellite television, and so on. The belief guiding these efforts is that all people are inherently good; that if they can merely know the truth, their consciences will steer them toward justice.

But persuading Chinese citizens to not be complicit in the persecution is a difficult task. Decades of political campaigns have the Chinese citizenry that the best course of action is to lay low, to keep one's head down, to follow orders, lest they also be targeted. Falun Gong's challenge is to convince people to put justice, and for the possibility of a better future ahead of their short-term interests. The best way we know to do that, from our own experiences in labor camps and detention centers, is to appeal to people's connection to eternal truths and virtues; to things which are lasting, and greater than any one of us.

And so, while the efforts to encourage renunciation from the Communist Party may appear politically driven, look closer and you will find that the message is not that Falun Gong should be in power, or that democratic revolution should be fomented. The message is that virtue and integrity—the cornerstones of China's Confucian and Buddhist traditions—must return to China. The message is that China's greatness, and the value of the Chinese people, lies precisely in the value that its culture places on moral courage, on compassion, and on justice.

I began by addressing how we understand the origins of the persecution against Falun Gong in China, and I will conclude by sharing how we hope it might end. If you ask a Falun Gong practitioner in China what they would do if freedom of belief were afforded to them, they will probably tell you that they'd like to go back to practicing meditation in the parks in the morning. They don't want political power, even after all that has transpired. And the way we hope to bring this about is by convincing the people of China that their greatness as a country and as a people is not based on their money, or their power projection. Their value comes from the fact that they are a people of justice and compassion. They are a people who will not stand by passively as their neighbors are imprisoned and tortured, and are a people who can sacrifice short-term interests in defense of what is right. In our best-case scenario, the persecution will end when the Chinese people decide that they are better than this.

○